Tony/

A few basic concepts
that companies fail
to execute.

Mapping Information Technology... to Your Business

Seven Initiatives for Creating and Understanding a Professional Information Technology Organization

Fred Mapp

1st WORLD LIBRARY
The World's Publisher

Austin, Texas

Mapping Information Technology ... to Your Business
Seven Initiatives for Creating and Understanding a Professional Information
Technology Organization
By Fred Mapp

©Fred Mapp, 2004
Mapping Information Technology ... to Your Business
Seven Initiatives for Creating and Understanding a Professional Information
Technology Organization

F&F Publishing
1st World Library
7600 Burnet Road, Suite 510
Austin, TX 78757
512-339-4000
www.1stworldlibrary.com

Library of Congress Control Number: 2004111953
ISBN: 0-9745624-4-0

First Edition

Senior Editor
Jill Gambon

Editors
Barbara Foley
Bob Mahoney
Brad Fregger

Cover Design
Jeff Koke, Koke Creative

Interior Layout Design
Amy Nottingham-Martin

For my wife Sandie—you have supported and encouraged me through all my professional aspirations. Through your constant love, inspiration, and sacrifice, you are the kindest and most thoughtful person I know. This is for you, Babe.

Acknowledgements

First, I would like to thank Jack Howell, who believed in me during my days at IBM and gave me the opportunity to attain a higher level of professional success. He presented me with challenges and offered me his priceless wisdom, which helped me grow and move forward in my career.

I am indebted to Bill Sanders, who was instrumental in helping me understand the importance of fulfilling customers' business needs and exceeding their expectations. Bill also helped foster my understanding of the benefits of IT governance and the need for business and IT alignment. His advice was essential to my demonstrating that there is indeed value in IT.

I would also like to acknowledge Jill Gambon's careful editing, advice, and input; this book is much better because of them.

Thanks to my publisher Brad Fregger and his outstanding editors who have helped make this book all that it can be.

Finally, I owe a great deal of thanks to all the people I have met and worked with over the years who provided knowledge and experience that contributed to my success. Without that exposure this book would not have been possible.

My sincere appreciation,

Fred

Foreword

Many would say change in our world eventually circles back to its beginning. In other words, if one waits long enough, what began as a new approach will eventually return to its origin. This is evident in our world economies, stock markets, and various vertical industries. All these things, despite the vicissitudes of business cycles, have attributes built on common fundamentals.

The same holds true for the Information Technology (IT) industry. The continuous introduction of new technologies and constant customer demand for real-time business value indirectly create the same cyclical phenomenon. Throughout these cycles, however, the one unchanging fundamental for IT leaders is the need to align IT strategies and goals with their company's business strategies and goals.

In *Mapping Information Technology ... to Your Business*, Fred Mapp shares the knowledge and expertise gained in more than 35 years of professional experience, providing information that can help protect IT leaders from getting caught up in these cycles. Fred's Seven Initiatives for Creating and Understanding a Professional IT Organization outline the fundamental principles for extracting more value from IT organizations and positioning IT as a true enabler of business success. Given today's corporate demands to produce immediate returns on IT investments, Fred's step-by-step approach lays out the blueprint to positively impact top- and bottom-line financials.

I have known Fred for almost two decades and have observed his personal mastery in applying the Seven Initiatives in a variety of settings. At IBM Corporation, Fred successfully implemented his Initiatives in the software services business, which helped increase revenue and improve customer value. Today, as I meet many of Fred's colleagues and industry peers, I hear them describe their success with the Seven Initiatives. In the rapidly evolving technology industry, the Initiatives are as relevant now as they were when Fred initially developed them.

Fred is truly a visionary. He has a unique gift to develop and execute a shared vision within the constraints and pressures facing IT organizations. His track record is built on proven success and results, which has earned him much respect and credibility within the IT profession.

I highly recommend *Mapping Information Technology ... to Your Business* to anyone looking to add immediate IT value to their business.

Douglas Ash
Vice President, Information Technology Solutions
Lockheed Martin Corporation
May 2004

Table of Contents

Acknowledgements   i

Foreword   iii

Table of Contents   v

Introduction   1

Initiative 1: Align IT Strategies with Your Organization's Vision,
Objectives, and Business Strategies   11

Initiative 2: Understand Your Company's Business Processes
so You Can Optimize IT's Role   25

Initiative 3: Mapping IT Infrastructure and Applications to Support
Your Business Needs   45

Initiative 4: Recruit, Develop, and Retain the Right Team   63

Initiative 5: Use Relationship Management to Provide Solutions
through Leadership, Consulting, and Communication   85

Initiative 6: Manage Costs across the IT Organization   101

Initiative 7: Measure the Success of Your IT Strategies   127

Summary: Bring the Initiatives to Life   145

About the Author   153

Introduction

What Is This Book About?

During my 35 years in the Information Technology (IT) profession, I have witnessed the incredible evolution of technology and have seen firsthand how it transformed business. I've seen industry's perception of IT evolve from a corporate backwater to a critical driver of innovation, efficiency, and success. Yet, despite all the gains, over the years I have often watched companies, both large and small, struggle with common challenges time and time again. More often than not, these challenges were not technology problems; they were basic business issues, such as developing effective processes, communicating organizational needs and goals, and recruiting and retaining the right team of people to attain success.

With this book, my goal is to share insights I've gained in the trenches and chart a course for businesses that will wring maximum value from their technology investments. The foundation for this book and an associated course are Seven Initiatives I developed and implemented at several companies, initiatives that helped drive these organizations forward. They are grounded in the basic principle of aligning IT strategies and investments with overarching business strategies and goals. These initiatives offer guidelines that any organization can adapt to its unique needs, whether it be a global corporation, a medium-sized business, a government agency, or a nonprofit organization.

In these pages I will also shed light on the much-debated topic of the value of Information Technology. Is it real or illusory? Through both the concepts and the processes that I describe in the Seven Initiatives, I will provide a framework that organizations can employ to reap significant value from their technology investments.

Not Just for Technocrats

This book addresses the key issues facing a range of IT professionals, from the Chief Information Officer (CIO) of multibillion-dollar multinational corporations to IT managers charged with shaping an IT department or organization, irrespective of size.

However, this book is not only for technocrats; it's also for professionals who work outside of IT and want to better understand the role it plays in their organization and who want to build better partnerships with IT. The Seven Initiatives covered in this book can apply to any occupation or business. If you are in finance, sales, human resources, marketing, or run a product line, this book touches on issues relevant to you, since we all face similar challenges in meeting business requirements.

The Business Value of IT: The First Test

If you're trying to measure the business value that IT delivers to your company, a first step is to assess how IT is viewed within your organization.

Ask this of any CIO or IT manager, and you'll hear a familiar refrain. Typically, in good times, they'll report that they are viewed as high-tech heroes who roll out new applications, devise innovative processes, and troubleshoot problems. When business conditions get rough, however, support for IT seemingly disappears. Then, if IT fails to provide adequate service due to cost constraints and then requests money for new projects, the partnership with the business units starts to unravel. This type of situation creates frustration on all sides as IT managers find themselves having to justify support costs, or explaining the implications of foregoing a new application or technology platform, or warning of the consequences if service levels are reduced because of inadequate funding. The challenge for everyone is to build the relationships, create the processes, and demonstrate the return on investment that is needed to sustain support for IT investments, in good times and in bad. The Seven Initiatives provide a road map to accomplishing these goals.

What Are the Facts?

Corporations today face their greatest challenges ever. During the past few years they have downsized, right-sized, and implemented a myriad of cost-cutting strategies to remain competitive. At the same time, companies still had to try to increase market share, improve the quality of their products and services, and keep customers satisfied. A variety of management programs have popped up, such as re-engineering, Total Quality Management, the Malcolm Baldrige National Quality Program, and ISO 9000, to help companies achieve their goals. In addition, companies spend billions on Enterprise Resource Planning, Customer Resource Management, and various other high-octane applications to deliver timely information necessary for making critical decisions.

While these initiatives can be costly and time-consuming to implement, many have proven absolutely necessary for remaining competitive. I have been involved with the rollout of nearly all these applications and initiatives, and I can unequivocally say that it takes a huge effort to get all the stakeholders on board. But make no mistake—for these programs to succeed, IT must be a key enabler, a facilitator, for making the necessary happen.

Spreading the Word

When I speak at CIO conferences, I often begin by posing a question to the audience: "What do you think is the *true* value of IT?" A long pause usually follows before anyone offers a response. Why the pause? Because many people in IT are unaccustomed to being asked this question. We often assume everyone knows our value. IT's true value is really not the issue. The issue is our perceived value; that's the basis upon which decisions are made. And, as I stated previously, perceived value can vary widely based upon the good times versus the bad.

My answer is that the *potential* value of IT is enormous, yet largely unrealized. IT can help an organization achieve extremely ambitious goals. It can drive an organization into new markets and it can create a competitive advantage. Yet, sometimes IT investments don't yield such results. Despite all the money spent on technology and new applications in pursuit of promised performance improvements, some IT departments fail to deliver their potential. Why?

True business value is sometimes difficult to gauge. We have all seen spectacular examples of IT in action, including expansive projects to implement ERP applications, e-business initiatives, firewalls that will withstand a nuclear attack, and the list goes on. IT does much more than just support the infrastructure but, unfortunately, many people don't see this. To foster a better understanding of the role that IT can play, IT executives and managers must better communicate the added value they bring to their organizations. An essential part of this process is working with colleagues outside of IT to learn how IT can best serve the organization's overall goals and to agree on how best to measure the return on all IT investments.

The Promised Land

Over the years, I've encountered many challenges in running IT. I always responded by applying fundamental business practices and processes to govern the use of technology. The biggest problem, in my experience, stems from the approach to managing IT. Too often, technology becomes the alpha and the omega of what we do. The quest for technology overwhelms other processes and obscures the need for proper business practices. And when this technology-for-technology's-sake approach falls short, IT looks ahead to the next release or product upgrade to lead it out of trouble and into the Promised Land. The truth is, when managing IT you must create your own Promised Land, or risk wandering forever in the corporate wilderness. Technology is only a tool—a walking stick, if you will—to help you reach your destination. Yet the best walking stick ever crafted won't find the way for you.

Seven Initiatives Overview

While working at IBM, Honeywell, AMD, and other companies, I have developed and refined a Seven-Initiative strategy of practices and processes to help steer organizations away from the siren song of technology-for-technology's sake. In the pages that follow, I'll offer practical, nuts-and-bolts advice for rolling out these initiatives. I hope that they provide a starting point for you.

Depending on your organization's structure and how it responds to change, some of the initiatives may suggest a radically different approach. In my experience, getting the support I needed wasn't always easy. But in every case, once these ideas were put into play, we achieved dramatic results. I have used these Seven Initiatives to help companies harness IT to achieve specific enterprise-wide business goals and objectives, including developing and retaining a talented team of professionals with top-notch technology and business skills, standardizing applications and platforms across a far-flung global company, and developing effective processes that contained costs. I believe that you, too, can use these initiatives to make an impact on your organization.

What are these initiatives? Here's a brief overview, before I discuss each on in depth.

Initiative 1: Align IT strategies with your organization's vision, objectives, and business strategies

Technology investments will be futile if they do not serve your organization's overarching goals and vision. As a first step, we will look at ways to assess how your IT strategies measure up and then, outline ways to bring them into alignment with the rest of your organization's goals and plans.

Initiative 2: Understand your company's business processes so you can optimize IT's role

Do sound business-process management principles guide your company? Does your IT organization routinely analyze your company's business processes to determine where IT can add value? This initiative will outline some of the tools IT organizations can use to evaluate and understand their company's business processes, which is the first step in planning improvements with IT.

Initiative 3: Mapping your IT infrastructure and applications to support your business needs

To get maximum value from your IT investments, you must fully leverage your underlying architecture. This begins with a careful analysis of your organization's activities and business processes and an examination of the applications required to support them. From this analysis, you can develop a strategic technology road map to guide all IT investments. This initiative will describe how to create a technology road map to ensure all IT spending and deployment serves current and planned business needs.

Initiative 4: Recruit, develop, and retain the right team

Whether the labor market is tight or flooded with talent, putting together a top-notch team is one of the biggest challenges facing IT managers. This initiative will cover such issues as fostering business savvy among technology professionals, determining the best mix of skills for the people on your team, and developing effective leadership.

Initiative 5: Use relationship management to provide solutions through leadership, consulting, and communication

Faulty software or defective hardware is not always the reason for the failure of major technology projects. Projects can crash and burn because the necessary relationships do not exist between IT and other parts of the business. Technology solutions can't be created in a vacuum. They must be crafted in partnership with the people who will use them. This initiative will suggest ways to forge and manage the relationships needed to develop technology solutions that respond to business requirements.

Initiative 6: Manage costs across IT

At one time or another, most IT managers have been given mandates to contain or cut spending. This initiative will describe processes for effectively planning and managing your IT budget to keep costs in line while delivering the solutions your organization needs.

Initiative 7: Measure the success of your IT strategies

No matter the size or scope of your organization's IT investments, you must track their effectiveness. What kind of return are you getting on your investments? How well is your IT strategy serving your customers, both your coworkers who use technology to do their jobs, and outside parties who pay for your products and services? This initiative will offer guidance for taking measure of your success.

Figure 1 shows how the Seven Initiatives process flows to support the business, providing value both individually and collectively.

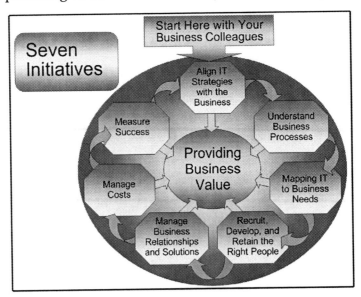

Figure 1

But First, a Few Ground Rules

Here are a few key points to bear in mind as you consider the Seven Initiatives:

1. Each Initiative must have an owner, someone in your IT organization who takes responsibility for it. Having a member of the IT executive or leadership team accountable is a key to success. The objective is to eventually have the Initiatives become part of the fabric of your organization; assigning accountability sets the stage for this to happen.

2. You must identify and integrate metrics to measure success. Without a demonstrable return on investment, it is nearly impossible to understand and communicate your value.

3. As you plan and develop new applications or platforms, be sure to involve the people who will use them. Their input and buy-in will be vital to the success of any project.

4. Involve your company's management team in any Initiatives. They can provide crucial insight and their support is necessary for success.

5. Execute, execute, execute on all the Initiatives.

Back to Basics

Some of this material may sound like basic, common sense. Keep in mind that my objective is to have you look at the big picture with a slavish devotion to gaining an understanding of the business problems you are trying to solve. In my travel I continue to find that neglecting business basics is a major problem in some IT organizations. You can't just throw technology at people without understanding their basic wants and needs and without having a grasp of their business requirements and goals. My

Seven Initiatives focus on how to tackle the issues in an orderly manner and create a structure that prevents the reoccurrence of these problems in the future.

Each Initiative chapter ends with a section titled: *Objectives, Strategies, and Metrics.* These provide examples of how the corresponding Initiatives can be implemented. You can use this material as a guide to help map IT to support your specific business needs.

Initiative 1

Align IT Strategies with Your Organization's Vision, Objectives, and Business Strategies

Alignment – What Does It Mean?

One of the most popular phrases you hear in IT is "alignment with the business." It's a catchy phrase, but what does it really mean, and how do you make it happen? Quite simply, it means that you execute all IT investments and initiatives to help advance the organization's overall goals and objectives; that every dime you spend on IT—whether for software, hardware, or services—is spent to solve a business problem; and that you must develop all IT initiatives to fulfill the requirements of the people who will use them.

Each one of the Seven Initiatives in this book offers guidance on how to align IT strategies with your organization's broader strategies and goals. One thing to bear in mind is that alignment always begins with a deep and thorough knowledge of your customers, whether they are your coworkers who use IT to do their jobs or your external customers who pay you for goods or services. You must understand their goals and objectives and what they need to do to achieve them. To develop that kind of knowledge, you will need strong relationships with your coworkers in finance, sales, purchasing, manufacturing, and human resources. By understanding what your colleagues do and what they require to accomplish their goals, you will be able to develop IT solutions to support them. As you build these relationships, it's important to remember that communication, and not just technology, is their foundation. Asking the right questions, understanding your coworkers' needs, and articulating your IT vision and strategies to those outside of IT are all crucial to the alignment process.

What's the Overall Direction for Your Company?

Successful companies have in common the development and communication of an overall strategy road map to define where they are going and what they are trying to achieve. This map consists of the vision, mission, objectives, and strategies needed for success. Not only does such a road map clearly define where the company is heading, it also serves as a common reference point for employees and customers, so everyone involved with the company is reading from the same page.

The underlying foundation of any road map is a clearly defined vision for your company. When I was at IBM, we had an initiative called "New Dimensions" and at American Express it was "Making the Blueprint a Reality." Often companies use the process of creating these blueprints to train management and build support from employees. Does your business have its own version of a company-wide vision or road-map program? If not, how do employees relate to what your company's leaders are trying to achieve? For example, how do you know what takes priority—growing revenue or increasing market share? A company-wide plan is essential to show what needs to be done, who needs to accomplish it, and how to measure results.

The Corporate Vision System is a model for delineating the direction an organization will take. It can be used to define a company's objectives and the strategies needed to achieve those objectives, as well as the corresponding IT-related objectives and strategies. It also outlines metrics and describes what is expected from the people who make it all happen. Once you define and articulate your organization's vision, you can design a road map.

Figure 2 is an example of a Corporate Vision System and shows how organizational and operational objectives are tied together. For a vision or plan to be successful, there must be a direct link between the vision and the individual contributor.

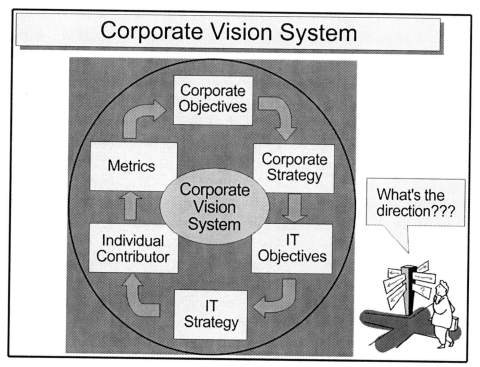

Figure 2

Get a Seat at the Table

Whenever your company is defining or refining its vision, IT must be involved. If you don't participate in direction-setting meetings for your company, you won't have a complete picture of its overall objectives. You'll be like the tip of an arrow—you won't have much influence on direction, but you will hit the wall first.

In the past, IT typically reported to executives like the Chief Financial Officer; this put IT management out of the loop, receiving news of corporate strategies and initiatives secondhand. This arrangement is akin to the childhood game of Telephone, where children sit in a circle, whisper a sentence one to another, and then marvel at the end how much the message gets distorted. By having a seat at the table with executives from other divisions of your company, you will have a full understanding of what your company needs from IT, and you'll be able to provide insight into how IT can drive forward the company's goals.

Throughout much of my executive career, I've been fortunate to be a member of the operating committees at the companies where I've worked. This has allowed me to collaborate with other executives to build business strategies from the ground up. When I was at Honeywell, for instance, we launched a project to look into the future to try to determine what role IT would play in it. It was called "Vision 2005+." The project team was charged with looking at all aspects of the business and at the impact IT had on it. One finding concluded that some of the company's IT organizations were disconnected from the business strategies and not adequately represented at policy-making committees. The project team felt that the overall corporate culture fostered a perception of IT as a cost function instead of a strategic weapon. At the time, my position as the VP of Information Technology did not report to the chief operating officer or president of the company, which contributed to the disconnect between IT and the business units. The company adopted the recommendation that the corporate CIO report directly to the company's president and the business unit CIOs report to the presidents of their respective divisions. This helped improve communication and made it easier to synchronize efforts between IT and the company's many divisions.

If you're not currently involved in the high-level goal- and strategy-setting sessions at your company, how do you get yourself included? Initially, getting a seat at the table may seem like trying to join some kind of secret society: mysterious, inaccessible, and beyond your reach. Don't panic. There are plenty of strategies for gaining access to the club. Start with the facts. Gather information about the impact that IT can have on your company. Look at what your competitors are doing with IT and demonstrate how it benefits them. Take this intelligence to one of your company's leaders. You need to find an advocate for IT who can go to bat for you and lobby for IT. Once you demonstrate the value that IT can add to your company, my guess is that you'll gain support.

What Are Your Company's Objectives?

As you establish IT as a player in your company's policy-setting processes, you will need to think beyond technology to the key business challenges facing your company. As part of this process, you will need to understand the top five or ten objectives that your company needs to accomplish. As you do that, you must consider the steps necessary to align corporate and IT objectives and then formulate a plan for communicating to your team their tasks ahead. Involving individual contributors such as project leaders, business analysts, and software engineers who actually do the work is critical. The earlier you bring in these folks, the better your chance for success. Involving them in the development of IT objectives that support the corporate plan makes the task of establishing IT's functional objectives, strategies, and metrics a whole lot easier.

As an example, suppose your company's objective is to eliminate legacy systems by combining the disparate applications employed by sales, finance, and procurement. The first step would be for IT to identify the technology objectives necessary to support this corporate objective. Having project leaders, business analysts, and other individual contributors help identify the project's business requirements and design the necessary processes from the get-go, can help eliminate confusion, reduce misinformation, and avoid delays.

What Is the Corporate Strategy?

Once the company determines its objectives, the next step is to define the strategies needed to achieve them. Those strategies may involve acquiring other companies, building market share, or expanding a company's geographic reach. Whatever strategies your company pursues, a common denominator will be that IT can contribute to all of them. And your IT organization has a major role to play in working with coworkers from finance, manufacturing, human resources, and various other parts of your company to bring these strategies to fruition. Your work must be tightly integrated with the efforts of colleagues from across your organization. Though your responsibilities may vary greatly, you are united in your pursuit of common goals.

From the Corporate Vision to the Vision for IT

Once your company has developed its organizational vision, objectives, and strategies, you will need to support them with corresponding vision, objectives, and strategies for IT. As you develop the vision, mission, and objectives, remember that they should be easy to communicate and easy to understand. At corporations where I have worked, we established a vision system supported by a practical, actionable strategy and instituted metrics to check progress. In every instance, constant communication with employees was the key to success.

Talk to Technology Users

As many organizations develop their vision and strategies for IT, a common shortcoming is a lack of skilled communicators. IT managers often fail to convey IT's potential value and they also fail to listen to what people around the company need from IT. How do you change this? Talk to managers, users of technology, and everyone in between. Show them what you do for them. Poll them. Ask them what they like, what they don't like, and what they need from IT. The information you gather may be eye-opening. And you'll not only educate yourself, but you are also likely to raise awareness about the services you provide.

Working as a consultant a few years ago, I was called in to find out why a company's customer-care personnel weren't using the expensive new software package the company had installed. I sat down with the users and asked them why the software was gathering virtual dust. Their response? "This new software stinks and nobody asked if we wanted it or what our requirements were." Decision makers up the corporate ladder had completely left the users of the software out of the loop, so it should have been no surprise when the users didn't support the changes.

The technology solutions you provide must have the technology user or customer at the center, rather than at the periphery. "Customer-centric" is a term that has gained much currency in recent years, but what does it really mean? It means you need to fully understand your customers' requirements so you can embed them within your tactical, strategic, and implementation plans. And again, by customer, I mean your colleagues whom you serve by developing and implementing IT solutions. Any world-class organization puts customers at the core of its strategies and solutions. Quite simply, there is no substitute for having a laser-like focus on the customer.

Meeting Users' Needs

Too often, people in IT fall in love with technology-for-technology's sake. The result is a situation where users find the deliverables are one-size-fits-none. Users find themselves with a load of cool tools that have no relevance to their business needs. If the IT organization provides all kinds of technology but not the right technology, users will often buy their own solutions from the local electronics store or by hiring consultants. This is the start of what I call *shadow* IT; that is, an organization doing IT-type work but not reporting to IT. Shadow IT projects could be as simple as a spreadsheet for tracking employee activities or as complex as a customized ERP application. Either way, it means unplanned applications, servers, or databases that need support. Ask any CIO or VP of IT and he or she will confirm that this can happen in the best-disciplined corporations. When these renegade IT projects or groups rise up, they create a variety of headaches for IT managers and ultimately for the rest of the company.

As a point of departure for our alignment-with-the-business discussion, let's first look at my model for meeting technology users' needs. Figure 3 displays business needs on one axis and IT investments on the other. The objective is to find the sweet spot between the two.

If you are meeting the needs of your users, you will find the sweet spot between business requirements and the implementation of technology. There are many factors involved in striking the right balance. To begin the process, these questions must be considered:

↬ Is the technology strategic?

↪ Do the business units understand the IT strategy for systems integration and the need for standardization of applications and hardware?

In this process, if business needs are not fully considered, then you end up with technology and/or IT solutions that users won't touch. Likewise, if IT doesn't have a significant role in the process, you are likely to end up with applications or platforms that run counter to your overall IT standardization and integration plans. As a result, you'll have spent a ton of money on new applications or systems that don't work with what you already have in place.

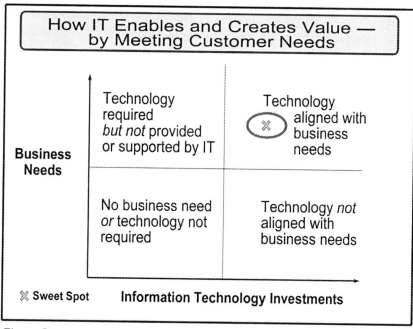

Figure 3

Do You Need to Change the Way You Manage Technology?

As you develop IT solutions to meet your users' business requirements, you need to consider how your organization manages technology. Does the way you manage IT allow for maximum alignment with the business? One challenge is to avoid the trap of focusing on new technologies at the expense of your company's objectives. You need to think instead about inventing and implementing new business models enabled by technology that will set your company apart from the competition. Amazon.com and Dell Inc. are companies that leveraged technology to come up with entirely new ways of doing business. What new business model awaits your company?

As new technologies develop, consider this question: Will this technology enable a stronger business model, or are you simply racing to replace the old version? Filtering unnecessary technologies is almost as important as implementing the right ones.

Formalize the Investment Prioritization Process

In many companies, the demand for IT-based solutions, whether they are new customer resource management applications or more advanced email platforms, will exceed the money and staff required to fulfill them. To decide which requirements are the most important, you need a prioritization process that allows a disciplined review of the company's goals and objectives and the possible technology investments that might serve them.

One way to formalize a prioritization process is through the establishment of a Business Technology Board, a panel responsible for reviewing requested IT projects and weighing them against the company's overarching strategies and goals. Typically, a board like this would be made up of a representative of IT, someone from your company's finance division, and people from other areas of the company. Such boards usually convene quarterly to review any changes in business strategies and set priorities for IT investments. As part of this process, you should divide your IT projects between strategic and tactical activities. Strategic IT investment should carry the weight and value of any research and development project, while tactical investments should continually be weighed against out-sourcing alternatives.

Strategic IT investments should be evaluated with a standard cost-benefit model that can be measured and tracked over time. To ensure a methodical, disciplined approach, I recommend that the Business Technology Board take ownership for developing the cost-benefit model and enforcing its use.

Communicate Your Vision

Several years ago when I worked at IBM, our organization submitted an application for an award to the Malcolm Baldrige National Quality Program. One section of the application asked how company leaders communicated the corporate vision to employees. When evaluators from the Baldrige program came on site to evaluate the application, I noticed they often talked to employees in the halls or cafeteria. Their objective was to determine what the employees knew about the company's overall direction. If the employees didn't know the corporate vision, goals, or strategies, the company failed the assessment of that section. The message was clear: an organization's vision must be communicated throughout the ranks or it is useless.

The same message holds true for those of us in IT. All employees, not just employees of IT, must understand that IT is critical to the company's future. IT should communicate its strategies to all levels of management to help the entire organization understand them. Employees need to understand their roles in turning these strategies and goals into reality. One way to make clear what is expected of employees is through regular communication and planning sessions, where managers discuss objectives and strategies and the employees work with management to develop action plans. I usually hold such sessions quarterly and convene special meetings to cover any important topics, such as a review of the corporate vision system.

I saw the benefits of such sessions when I worked at Honeywell. With the company's senior management team I conducted sessions with the IT employees to explain the corporate vision, objectives, and strategies and to obtain their participation and support. We discussed our business colleagues' objectives and strategies, and what they were doing to execute their plans. Next, we asked participants in the session to put together an action plan and describe what they would do to ensure the business successfully met the objectives. We asked that they focus on what they could do differently than was currently being done, and on what would be required to meet the business objectives.

I must admit I was surprised to discover that some in the room did not understand the connection between their company's business objectives and the company's dependencies on IT to achieve those objectives. Explanations were needed, as was some convincing. Overall, this exercise proved to be useful because the IT employees became more involved with and finally understood the company's business problems and what they had to do to help solve them. They also came to understand where IT had to focus and the importance of prioritizing projects that supported the business objectives.

Some Questions to Consider

As you align your business and IT strategies, ask yourself these questions to assess where you stand now and how well positioned you are to move forward.

1. Does your company expect IT's strategy to be explicitly linked to company-wide business strategies and initiatives?

2. Do your company's top executives expect the stakeholders within the business units (i.e. the employees who will use IT to do their jobs) to prioritize IT initiatives based on their expected benefits? Should business-unit managers sponsor or lead approved technology initiatives?

3. Should the business units be accountable for realizing the financial or operational benefits that are proposed as part of the justification for IT projects?

4. Does your company's leadership expect IT to regularly measure and report on the project's performance?

5. Do your company's leaders expect IT to promote awareness of emerging technologies and to advise business managers of technology alternatives?

6. Does your company expect IT to approve the acquisition of technology resources that conform to architectural standards?

If you answer "No" to any of these questions, you are likely to encounter obstacles to achieving maximum alignment between your business and IT strategies. The following initiatives, however, provide guidance on how to overcome the hurdles you face.

Objectives, Strategies, and Metrics for Initiative 1

Align IT strategies with your organization's vision, objectives, and business strategies.

Objectives

- ↳ Communicate the company and IT vision to all employees.

- ↳ Align IT objectives and strategies with business objectives and strategies.

- ↳ Ensure IT enables and creates value by understanding business requirements.

- ↳ Formalize the investment prioritization process.

Strategies

- ↳ Establish and implement a process for communicating the vision to all employees.

- ↳ Create a list of individual objectives and specific steps to fulfill the vision.

- ↳ Increase the visibility of IT to the company's executive staff and technology users.

- ↳ Establish a Business Technology Board review process.

Metrics

- ↳ Percent increase in knowledge of the corporate vision.

- ↳ Percent of participation and buy-in from employees.

- ↳ Reduced number of non-strategic projects and projects implemented outside of IT (Shadow IT).

Initiative 2

Understand Your Company's Business Processes so You Can Optimize IT's Role

Know How Your Company Works

As you work to align your IT strategies with your company's business strategies and goals, a key step is to understand the business processes that your company uses in sales, finance, human resources, manufacturing, and elsewhere. Only by understanding how and why work gets done can you figure out ways to improve things through IT.

In recent years, companies across the globe have focused huge amounts of time, energy, and money on business-process re-engineering because of the potential upside it can bring. IT's role as an enabler in these efforts is pivotal, paving the way for significant improvements in cycle time, quality, and driving down costs.

In the upcoming pages, we'll look at ways to analyze and understand business processes as a first step to building the IT strategies that will provide maximum value to your organization. Tools such as a business-process review and a current-state assessment will help you understand what processes you have, where room for improvement exists, and how IT can help. I will also define a framework for IT governance, a system that will instill a disciplined, rational approach to all IT development and investment. IT governance, which is becoming increasingly common in large corporations, can fit small and mid-sized businesses, too, as well as public-sector agencies and nonprofits.

Business Process Review

Once your company has developed a vision for the future and communicated plans to the employees, the next step is to ensure the necessary processes are in place to support that vision. The identification and implementation of these processes will serve as the vehicle that moves your company toward its goals and objectives. To start, you'll need to examine the processes you have in place and assess how well they align with your company's overall business strategies. Are the processes obsolete? Do they make sense? Can they be streamlined? Once you take stock of where your company currently stands, you can begin to consider ways technology might bring improvements.

As your company identifies and reviews its business processes, it is important that all divisions of the company participate. Each division, such as sales, human resources, and finance, needs to identify its key processes and must ensure those processes are adequately documented so that all employees share the knowledge of what these processes are, how they are executed, and how they are measured.

Your company can pay big bucks to have outsiders assess its processes or it can conduct a review of its own. Either way, IT can play a huge role in gaining this understanding and in devising ways to improve the processes by investing in the right technology.

Start by Interviewing Key Executives

When I undertake a business-process review, my first step is to schedule some time with several key executives from various divisions of the company. I interview each one, asking about the processes their workers use, how effective those processes are, and where they need improvement. For example, when I meet with the head of sales, I typically ask the following questions:

- What is your business process for revenue generation?

- Is that process documented and shared among your employees?

- How long is the sales cycle and what segments of it are the most time-consuming?

- What segments of the sales cycle do you think could be simplified by technology?

Talking through these questions is a perfect gateway for a discussion about how IT can provide business value and where it can help boost productivity or cut costs.

I also bring for discussion a chart, as displayed in Figure 4, that describes examples of the company's overall high-level processes. This tool often spurs discussion about the processes in each business unit.

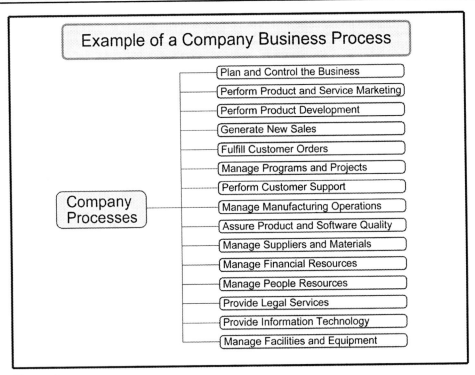

Figure 4

At another company, we were going to implement a new ERP (Enterprise Resource Planning) application. We applied this review process and obtained valuable input from the company's executive team. For instance, after reviewing his processes, the senior sales executive said his vision would be to have a sales portal where sales people could enter their forecast information and track sales-to-date, as well as any backlog. This would give the sales team the ability to forecast and track sales at any time, something they could not previously do.

The sales executive also believed it was important to track sales, expenses, and profits on a daily basis, or at least on a weekly basis, so the company would know how we were progressing throughout the quarter. He pointed out that some companies can close their books on a daily basis, which took us weeks at the end of a quarter. Based on his input, the IT organization was able to develop a solution that gave nearly real-time data on sales and inventory.

The bottom line is that this valuable input would not have been captured without an effective process for collecting requirements. This method also prepared us for the next step: decoding the business processes with people in the sales organization.

Decoding Your Business Processes

As you gather information about your company's various business processes, you need to break them down to understand them in detail. To demonstrate, let's examine the process of generating new sales, a standard process for any sales team.

Figure 5 displays the deconstruction of a "Generating New Sales" process.

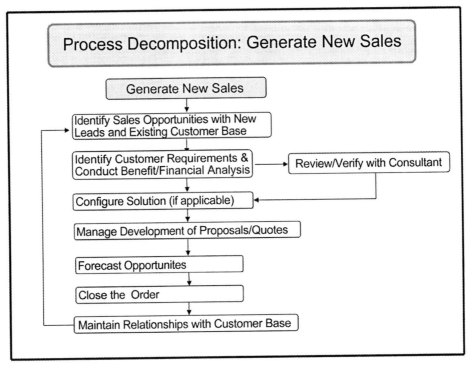

Figure 5

As you can see, there are many opportunities where the implementation of technology, such as a customer relationship management (CRM) application, can apply. By breaking down these key processes into discrete parts, not only will you fully understand what goes into them, you'll also be able to devise ways that IT can improve them.

One cautionary note: As you undertake a business-process review, you must balance the competing demands of a detailed and thorough analysis with the need for simplicity. Be on guard for "analysis paralysis," a state where the organization is so tied up in self-evaluation that progress comes to a screeching halt. Staying focused on your objective and keeping the work simple is a far better route.

Current-State Assessment

Once you've identified your company's business processes, you have to analyze their effectiveness. You need to identify any shortcomings, whether they are in the processes themselves or in the links between the processes and the technology required to support them. Once you've identified any areas for improvement, you can begin to formulate detailed action plans—including specific deadlines—to close the gaps.

How do you develop the necessary level of understanding about your business processes? How do you really know what is effective and what is lacking? I conduct what I call a "current-state assessment," during which the current IT strategic plan is evaluated in the context of the company's broader business objectives. This project involves people from every division or business unit and will ultimately answer the question: Does the existing IT architecture support the business processes currently in place?

As you do this, you need to ask yourself: Which processes are documented and which ones need to be documented? Are the processes effective? Is there currently an application that supports these processes? To identify any gaps between the technology and your company's current or anticipated business needs, you need to look at your IT architecture, including the infrastructure and the applications. At both AMD and Honeywell, the current-state assessment teams reviewed the major applications, the underlying technology, the business requirements, and the processes. The teams surveyed employees to gauge their satisfaction with IT and developed an overall assessment of the company's IT systems.

The following page contains an example of a current-needs assessment checklist.

Current-Needs Assessment Checklist

❑ **Step 1 - Start-up and Preparation:** Develop and document initial project plans and staffing activities.

❑ **Step 2 - Current-State Assessment:** Perform an inventory of systems and multiple users. Survey the users and IT support personnel to establish overall quality and satisfaction levels.

❑ **Step 3 - Business Objectives:** Review, consolidate, and prioritize strategic goals, objectives, and business processes.

❑ **Step 4 - IT Principles:** Develop a set of guiding principles to be used for IT decision-making.

❑ **Step 5 - IT Architectures:** Develop high-level models of the applications, data, technology and organizational architectures.

❑ **Step 6 - IT Management and Organization:** Develop a conceptual framework for an IT organization required to support the rollout of a strategic IT plan.

❑ **Step 7 - Gap Analysis:** Identify the differences between current-state and future-state applications, technology, management, and organization, which will collectively define the potential scope of the work.

❑ **Step 8 - Strategic Initiatives Development:** Use the knowledge gained from the preceding stages to develop a portfolio of improvement initiatives and a high-level implementation plan.

❑ **Step 9 - Document the Results:** Share information about the project with the company's executive team.

Survey Your Technology Users

To help gather the necessary information, you'll need to survey key people within your company. I usually put together a simple questionnaire that I call a *Needs Assessment Survey.* As part of a business-process review several years ago, I circulated a 20-question survey to obtain data on more than a dozen major business processes. The survey included questions about both the business processes and the IT applications and infrastructure required to support them.

The responses were telling, pointing out several gaps between what the company needed from IT and what it was getting. From the survey we learned that nearly every business process was perceived to require significant IT support to function effectively. Though application investments had been made over the preceding years to support some processes, the pace of improvement had not kept up with overall demand. Consequently, many current needs were not being met due to missing or poorly integrated applications and business information.

Based on those findings, we made several recommendations for follow-up, including: prioritize IT investments to focus on a few key areas; make high-impact improvements to the technical infrastructure; propose an IT architectural road map to serve as an overall game plan; and create an IT Board to validate the road map, guide investment priorities, and monitor existing programs. That was a hefty agenda, to be sure, but the company never could have arrived at the point of knowing where it needed to go without a thorough and disciplined business-process analysis.

Walking the Walk: IT's Business Processes

Those of us in IT share responsibility for making sure that the business processes we use are effective and well documented. To stay focused on this, you need to continually ask yourself such questions as: Do I manage

IT as a business? What is the process for technology implementation once a project is approved and applications are selected? What business processes are used in the IT organization to ensure that applications are installed in a timely manner? What service levels do technology users expect?

Figure 6 is an example of an IT business-process model, displaying several processes that IT can use to support business requirements. Each process should have an objective, project name, owner, definition, and deliverables.

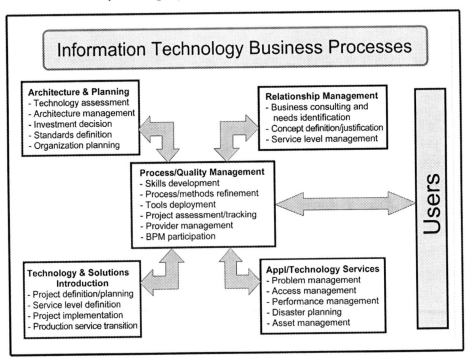

Figure 6

Taking that a step further, Figure 7 shows a breakdown of the Technology and Solutions process and sub-processes. By articulating the goals, objectives, ownership, and deliverables, you clearly define and communicate expectations, making the management and measurement of the processes much easier.

Managing Your Business Processes: Skills Required

It takes expertise to create new processes and manage projects. Do the people who work in IT at your company have process-management skills? Are they familiar with standards from such organizations as the Project Management Institute and the Software Engineering Institute? The Project Management Institute offers project-management education, training, certification, and professional standards. The Software Engineering Institute operated by Carnegie Mellon University focuses on software development quality and associated disciplines, including process management. Both organizations are invaluable resources for help and training in project and process management.

Technology and Solutions Introduction Processes

- Project Definition and Planning
- Service Level Definition
- Project Implementation
- Production Service Transition

Process Name: Project definition and planning.

Objective: To professionally manage the definition, planning, and implementation of approved IT projects to achieve their scope, schedule, and budget requirements and to effectively transistion the solution into the appropriate production environment.

Process Owner: Joe Project and Mary Leader

Process Definition: This process is to define and plan an IT project based upon requirements agreed to by the business. This phase is managed by the IT project manager and leader and its deliverable is a document of understanding which defines project objectives, cost benefits, scope, deliverables and their deadlines, and scope management.

Deliverable: Completed project plan for discussion with the business.

Figure 7

When your IT staff people are trained in process management, they'll understand the importance of documenting and measuring the effectiveness of your business processes. Without documentation, you're relying on memory and habits. Without metrics and measurements, you can't possibly know how effective you are or when you need to change course. We implemented PMI (Project Management Institute) standards at Honeywell and trained many who received process-management certifications. The payoff was obvious. The added skills made a significant impact on the success of our projects and on staff development. Good project-management discipline is absolutely essential to deliver projects on time and on budget.

Introducing IT Governance

Once you've established sound business processes for your IT organization, you need to formalize them so they become standard practice at your company. You need to put in place a structure and processes that allow the business units to set the direction for IT, and for IT to add value to your business with its expertise, knowledge, and skills. A way to accomplish this is by instituting a structure for IT governance.

An IT governance structure is a system of committees made up of key stakeholders and decision-makers within your company. These committees provide a framework for disciplined management and a forum for communication to address business-technology needs. IT governance is becoming increasingly common at many large companies where the need for disciplined, coordinated IT development and spending is critical.

Can IT Governance Really Improve the Bottom Line?

According to research by Gartner and the Massachusetts Institute of Technology (MIT), companies with above-average IT governance performance were more profitable. While governance was not the only factor contributing to the success of these companies, strong governance practices often came with effective management practices in all areas.

> The MIT research with Gartner EXP members found that firms with above average IT governance performance also had superior profits as measured by three-year industry adjusted return on assets (ROA). The differences varied by strategy of the firm, but the firms with the above-average governance had average ROAs more than twice the size of firms with poorer governance.
>
> *Gartner Research – Tailor IT Governance to your enterprise – October 2003*
> *Marianne Broadbent – Gartner*
> *Peter Weill - MIT*

Building a Governance Structure

The size of a company, the way it is organized, and the complexity of its business will dictate what kind of governance structure it needs. Smaller or medium-sized businesses, or nonprofit agencies, may just need committees to set the IT road map and to review "quick hitters," or relatively small-budget projects that need prompt evaluation. Multinational corporations with thousands of employees and diverse lines of business probably need a more elaborate governance structure. Bear in mind that the objective is to simplify the process of IT management, not to complicate it. Figure 8 shows an example of a governance structure for a fairly large corporation, while Figure 9 indicates how it can be customized to fit any size organization.

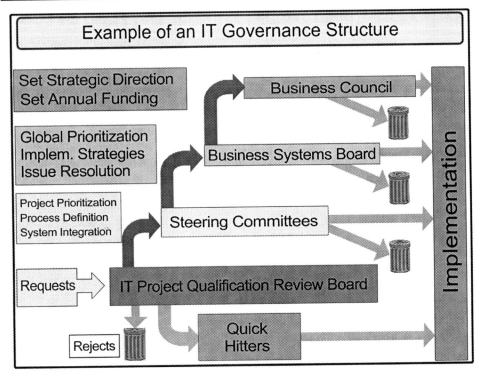

Figure 8

At the highest level is a Business Council made up of top finance and IT executives who review the total IT budget, the overall resource-allocation plan, and the global IT road map. Next, there is a Business Systems Board which reviews all requests for IT projects that require major investments or impact more than one area of the business. It consists of executives from various business units or divisions. Under this are a series of Steering Committees such as Quality, Finance, Purchasing, and Sales, assigned to review the progress of all IT projects, upgrades, and the architecture road maps that impact their particular area of the business. With this type of committee system, the business units become the primary decision-makers for the direction of IT projects and programs. Finally, a Qualification Review Board approves small fixes, upgrades, and quick projects requested by the business units and preapproves all projects submitted to the steering committee to make sure all necessary supporting information is in place.

The prospect of governance shouldn't make your eyes glaze over or raise fears of bottlenecked decisions due to added layers of management. On the contrary, when executed correctly, this structure can streamline your IT decisions. I will describe in more detail how these groups can work, what processes they can use, and the impact they can have. Remember, you can adapt this suggested governance framework to fit your company or organization.

I will offer one caveat about implementing a governance structure: limit the number of meetings to what is strictly necessary. Needlessly tying up people in meetings keeps them from getting their jobs done. When you do meet, follow a strict agenda, which will add discipline to the process and keep people on message and focused on the business problems you are trying to solve.

The Corporate Business Council

The Corporate Business Council's role is to address broad strategic issues that require senior-management approval. The council reviews the IT budget and makes recommendations on IT investment. The Council reviews the complete IT road map and makes sure that it supports the company's objectives. In addition, the council can provide a forum for the IT executives to communicate trends and new product development in the technology market. The council should be co-chaired by the company's CFO and CIO.

Business System Board

A Business System Board should be made up of vice-president-level executives from across the company and co-chaired by a director and an executive from one of the business units. The board approves projects that require large investments of money or resources, or that require commitment from more than one division or business unit. It also decides business-process issues that cannot be resolved by the steering committees. The Business System Board owns the IT road map for business applications. As with the Business Council, the board provides a forum for IT to bring information on technology trends to this particular group of executives.

The Steering Committees

The steering committees drive necessary changes to business processes to improve productivity and make progress toward company goals. The committees must be empowered to make quick decisions on upgrades and new projects that are within their financial authority. I recommend that each steering committee be made up of representatives from the respective business unit (i.e. Finance, Sales, etc.) and a person from IT. The number of members from the business units can vary, depending on the number of business processes involved. The executive of the business unit should select steering committee members. The group should include a chairman who is an executive from the business unit and who has final say on approval, deferral, or rejection of all items brought to the committee, and a facilitator, who is a senior manager from IT working on applications in the committee's line of business.

Each steering committee should review all IT projects on a monthly basis to ensure that they are on schedule, within budget, and will deliver on the promised goals. On a quarterly basis, the steering committees should review the IT application road map to track progress.

Qualification Review Board

The Qualification Review Board should be composed primarily of IT staff and chaired by an IT director. It approves smaller projects and upgrades and makes sure that all submissions to the steering committees are fully documented and make business sense. In addition to making decisions on resource allocation for smaller projects, the board reviews materials to be presented to the steering committee. This guarantees that submissions are complete and make technical and business sense.

Figure 9 is a less complex process flow showing how one could adjust the same structure for a smaller company. For example, the Business Council and Business Systems Board could become one entity, and the IT Project Qualification Review Committee could be a sub-committee of the single Steering Committee.

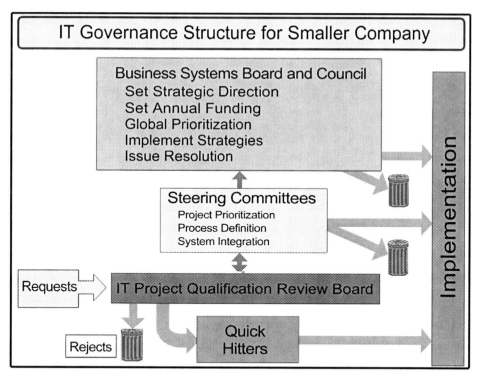

Figure 9

What's the Upside?

A growing body of research shows that the difference between the winners and losers in business is whether or not they have IT governance in place. As IT has become increasingly critical to success, IT-related decision-making has become more complex. CIOs can cut through the complexity by adopting IT governance models that best fit their company's goals. Quicker and smarter decisions about IT investments can lead to faster product development, swifter sales cycles, reduced costs, and better customer relationships.

In addition, by bringing business-process management principles and the discipline of good project-management skills into your IT organization, you'll be taking a big step forward in aligning yourself with your company's broader business strategies and corporate vision. That's something no one can afford to ignore.

Objectives, Strategies, and Metrics for Initiative 2

Understand your company's business processes so you can optimize IT's role.

Objectives

- Understand the business processes your company uses.

- Formalize, document, and measure all relevant processes.

- Improve old processes, and create new processes where necessary to fulfill your vision.

- Secure ownership and accountability for each business process.

Strategies

- Implement a process for current-state assessment and gap analysis of company processes.

- Use benchmarking, technology user review meetings, and user surveys to trigger process improvements.

- Encourage participation and provide feedback mechanisms for process improvement.

- Implement a governance structure to establish ownership and direction.

Metrics

- Percent increase in survey results of meeting users' needs.

- Include corporate objectives in IT performance plans.

- Percent of processes documented by the business function.

- Number of newly documented processes.

Initiative 3

Mapping IT Infrastructure and Applications to Support Your Business Needs

Getting Maximum Value from Your Technology Infrastructure

Businesses large and small, nonprofit organizations, and government agencies face a common charge: getting maximum value from their IT investments. The sobering climate of the post-technology boom has heightened the need for careful scrutiny of every penny spent on IT. The pressure to demonstrate return on investment (ROI) has never been greater for those involved in IT planning and management. As a result, companies of all sizes need to optimize their IT architectures by finding the best hardware, software systems, and applications that support the needs of their businesses. In other words, you need to map your technology plans to support your business requirements. To accomplish that, you need to develop road maps for both your technology infrastructure and for your applications that advance your business goals both now and in the future.

A technology road map will provide you with a thorough and well-articulated plan for software and hardware deployment that looks not just to the next quarter or the next fiscal year but two, three, or five years ahead. A well-crafted road map can guide all future IT investment, so any new hardware or software platforms will work with the technology already in place. Without a technology road map, it's nearly impossible to effectively coordinate plans for migrating from one technology platform to another, or to upgrade to a new software release.

Building on ground covered in Initiatives 1 and 2, Initiative 3 will step you through creation of the technology road maps you'll need to guide all IT planning and spending. These road maps can help rein in disparate systems, streamline data access, prevent shadow IT projects, and ensure a coordinated, disciplined approach to IT investment and deployment. In creating the necessary road maps, we'll explore the benefits of systems integration, examine the challenges of selecting the right hardware and software applications, and discuss methods for analyzing your company's applications portfolio.

Optimizing IT

How do you know if you're getting optimum value from your underlying IT architecture and from the software applications you use? To ascertain where you stand, start by asking yourself these questions:

> ✍ Is the company getting maximum use of its current hardware and software? Can the current IT architecture and applications scale to support future needs?

> ✍ Are there functionality or reliability gaps in the current software?

✍ What rationale is used when deciding whether to buy technology off the shelf or build it in house?

✍ Do the people in our company have easy access to the information they need to do their jobs effectively?

✍ Do the applications we have now fulfill business requirements?

The answers to these questions will help guide your priorities as you develop your strategic and application road maps.

First, Know Your Destination

Before you can begin any journey, you need to know your destination, or what I refer to as "the point of arrival." Before you start devising any technology road maps, you need to know where your company wants to go. At the highest level, this is laid out in the company's corporate vision, mission, and its strategic plans. On a more practical level, your destination for IT is articulated in your strategic technology plan. A point of arrival may be for IT to provide a consolidated view of all customer information, such as sales and service requests, that can be used to improve customer management and retention and to guide product development. Or, for a company that wants to improve field service, it might be the creation of a web-based interface that allows managers, service representatives, and customers to coordinate service requests. Ultimately, every decision you make about your intended destination should seek to answer the simple question: "What business problem am I trying to solve?"

Systems Integration: Bringing Order to Potential Chaos

Over the years, it has become increasingly clear that the value of data diminishes if it can't be accessed in a timely manner, then analyzed and used by the people who need it. Islands of information disconnected from the rest of the business represent underutilized assets.

Customer data has taken on increased significance as businesses have realized that intimate knowledge of customers and their business needs provides a competitive edge. The ability to listen to customer needs and deliver timely solutions has become as valuable as any corporate asset. Indeed, companies, especially those doing business globally, often require a seamless integration of all data relating to customers. For example, valuable customer information gathered through call centers, sales, marketing, and product staff is a critical resource that can be used to not only serve and retain customers but also generate new revenue. The challenge, however, is gathering this data and applying the right technology to centralize, effectively manage, and use it.

So how do you make data available to the right people in the format they need when they need it? Simply put: through systems integration. That means making sure every bit of new technology deployed is compatible with the systems currently in use. It means creating a methodical plan for migrating to new platforms so that data stored in legacy systems remains readily available. It means developing a single access point to data, so technology users in your company can turn raw data into corporate intelligence and your customers and suppliers save time and money doing business with you.

Figure 10 is an example of a plan for a systems-integration project. The intended destination here is a single point of access to information for all units of the company. The system should allow flexibility for change and support strategies such as e-business and any need for real-time reporting.

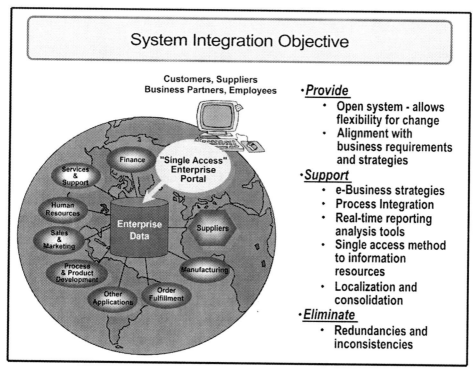

Figure 10

No matter the size of your company or your organization, I strongly recommend that any system-integration effort include a single-access enterprise portal to streamline data access. The objective of an enterprise portal is to allow people in your company to get finance, service, support, sales, marketing, and other data from a desktop, laptop, or PDA. Simple and instant data access will make it easier to align IT with changing business requirements and strategies, support accurate, real-time reporting and analysis, and streamline integration of business processes. Imagine the advantages of instant access to up-to-date shipping deadlines, quantities available, and all other information that customers require. The bottom line is that systems integration enables your organization to turn raw data into the valuable information that runs your business.

Building Support for Your Plans

To successfully execute systems integration, you must convince colleagues who work in other parts of your company—in finance, human resources, manufacturing, sales, and elsewhere—to support your goals. Everybody must row in the same direction to reach your intended destination.

How do you get everybody on board? You provide a thorough and convincing analysis of the benefits of a consolidated and standardized technology infrastructure. This kind of analysis is the product of a thoughtful examination of all business activities and the applications needed to support them. Consider if you really need all the software that is currently deployed in your company, whether it's ERP, financial applications, email platforms, or other products. Try documenting how all the disparate applications and systems affect business processes. How long does it take to close a sale? How long to give a customer a quote? Think about potential cost-savings. Could you get by with fewer servers and support personnel if you consolidated servers? How much money would that save? There are dozens of questions you can ask for every business function. Having a clear picture of the benefits of a consolidated, streamlined infrastructure will provide you with a powerful tool when it comes time to lobby for support. While some applications and servers may be justified as parts of fiefdoms within the company, having concrete numbers on your side can help you rationally evaluate your needs and support the decisions that you make.

What's in Your Portfolio?

As part of any systems-integration effort, you need to look at your applications portfolio. Typically, in large organizations you will find a truckload of applications and disparate systems from a variety of vendors as represented in Figure 11. Does this picture look familiar? How many different systems and applications do you have in your company?

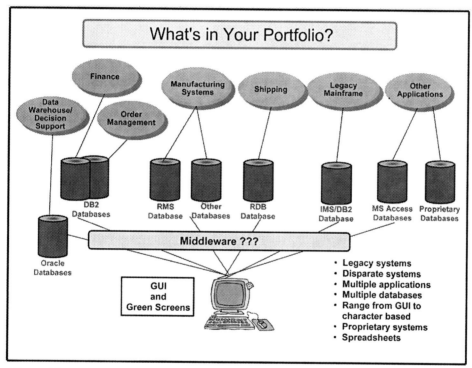

Figure 11

If your application portfolio looks something like Figure 11, you will probably find irksome incompatibilities among software applications, especially when it comes time to change something. Modifying code very likely means you need to invoke small armies of programmers to develop, implement, and maintain the interfaces that link various applications together. You also probably have redundant hardware, including the dozens of servers required to run all the applications. In recent years, many businesses have started waking up to the problems of underutilized servers. As a result, many IT shops have undertaken server consolidation in an effort to better utilize their existing processing capacity and rein in infrastructure sprawl.

Be Careful What You Wish For

As you undertake any systems integration effort, you need to be careful not to go overboard in bringing rigid uniformity to your IT architecture. You must maintain some flexibility to easily adapt to any changes in business processes or in market conditions. For instance, all business processes may not be adequately served with one vendor's application. Marketing claims notwithstanding, I have not seen one vendor who is best of breed in all categories of ERP, customer-relationship management, and supply-chain software. A mix-and-match of applications may be necessary, but try to use as few products as possible.

What Does It Take to Get a Report?

To demonstrate the benefits of systems integration, let's look at the hardware and applications involved in the generation of business reports. Most companies live or die by reviewing reports on current sales, costs, inventory, or other critical decision-making information. Think about this for a second:

↬ How many systems and applications does it take to generate a report for your business?

↬ How efficient is the process?

↬ What happens when you need to make changes to the reporting system?

At one company where I worked, we looked at report generation and found a jumble of applications, servers, and interfaces. Over the years, disparate applications and systems were implemented to meet customer requirements. Since no strategy or road map was followed, various servers and applications were purchased in house and interfaces had to be developed to kludge them all together.

Figure 12 shows both where we started and where we wanted to go. The left side displays how many different systems were used to generate reports when we started this process. The right side represents our road map for report generation as part of an optimized architecture. This process became part of a server-consolidation initiative to reduce costs. I call this "the many to the few" concept.

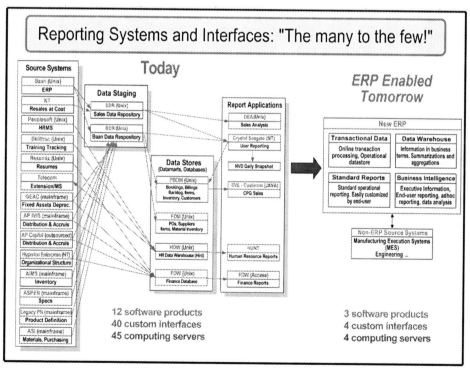

Figure 12

As you can see from the figure, we greatly reduced the number of servers and applications required to generate reports, dropping from 45 servers to 4; 40 custom-built interfaces to 4; and 12 different software products down to 3. The savings were significant and the entire reporting process became much more efficient.

Charting Your Business Processes and Applications

Mapping your company's various business processes and the applications that support them is an important component of building an optimized IT architecture. You have to know your current business applications as well as the possibilities and the limitations of your infrastructure before you can go about optimizing the infrastructure. Creating road maps for both applications and infrastructure will provide blueprints that guide all future IT spending.

To begin this process, I suggest creating a chart like Figure 13. First, try listing every business process, everything you do as an organization: sales, procurement, finance, order entry, human resources, etc. Then list the vendors and the applications that support each function. You may be surprised at the number of vendors and disparate applications required to support your business processes. The next step is to decide what applications will best support the business process *and* can also integrate them, especially if your strategy is to go from the many to the few.

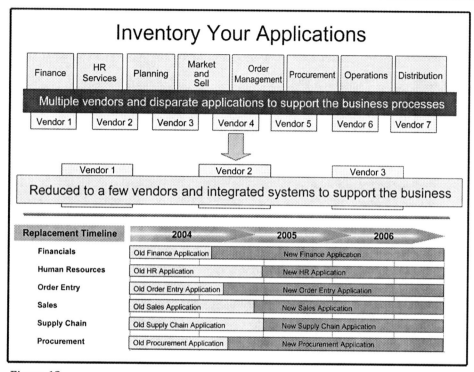

Figure 13

Creating an Infrastructure Road Map

Next, you need to map out plans for your infrastructure—the operating systems, chip technology, directory services, database systems, and other technology building blocks on which your company runs its business. As displayed in Figure 14, this road map will provide a clear picture of the status of each component of your infrastructure and display a timeline for upgrading or replacing it.

Each decision made about your architecture should support your business goals and should help advance the objectives in your company's strategic plan. For example, if your company were planning to improve database management to enhance the availability of critical business information, your infrastructure road map should reflect that by showing a migration to 32/64-bit technology in the related time frame. Again, you should chart plans for each component of your architecture from the present to three to five years in the future.

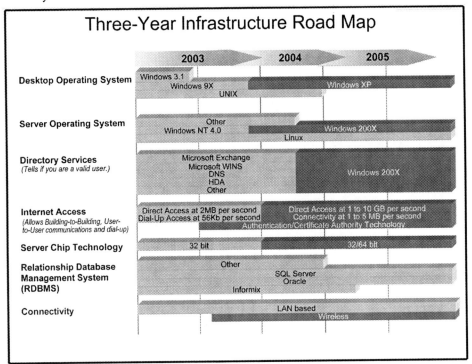

Figure 14

Following the Road Maps

Once you've created application and infrastructure road maps, people throughout your company need to follow them. If individual business units or divisions decide to build an IT application of their own or independently deploy a new handheld device, you'll end up with shadow IT—those unplanned, unbudgeted IT projects that suddenly need troubleshooting and support. How do you ensure everyone adheres to the guidance set out in the road maps? That's where IT governance structure comes into play. Depending on the governance structure in place, the Business Council or similarly empowered group should have the authority to ensure compliance with the plan.

To keep the road maps relevant, they should be reviewed at least twice a year, or when any major changes in your company's direction or strategy occur. Mergers, acquisitions, and shifting priorities such as cost containment and outsourcing will also require that adjustments be made. It's wise to maintain a degree of flexibility so you can respond to changing market or economic conditions or seize new opportunities for growth or improved productivity.

A Matter of Choice: Picking the Best Applications and Hardware

As you develop your technology road maps, consider the selection process for applications, systems, and hardware. Is there a methodical, documented process for mapping business requirements to hardware and software purchases, or do you wing it when it comes time to buy?

One method for product selection is by generating a Request for Proposals. This process will help organize a list of the features and functionality needed. For instance, if you were in the market for ERP software, you would begin the process by looking at your application road map and the corresponding business processes. From there, build a list of requirements for the software. With that list in hand, ask the vendors how their applications map to your requirements. Figure 15 depicts a comparison of the relative features and benefits in the selection process.

As displayed in the figure, you have to weigh the software features available today (shown in gray), and what the vendor is promising to deliver in the future (shown in black). Another variable considered here is whether the software's benefits are focused on your customers or your internal operations. Using the requirements defined in the Request for Proposals will keep you focused on selecting the best product to suit your needs.

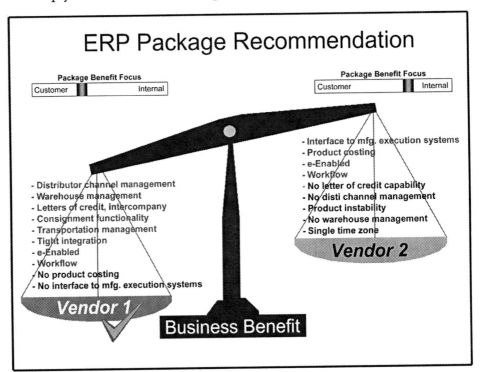

Figure 15

When Does IT Produce Value?

As your IT investment plans take shape with the development of the technology road maps, expectations for IT will rise. Not only will people within your company expect more value from IT, but outside parties, especially shareholders of publicly traded companies, will, too. They will demand return on technology investments and will want IT to fulfill its promise as a key enabler of business success. For people who work in IT, this creates the challenge of managing those expectations. Figure 16 is based on research from Gartner that shows a typical time lag between the investment in IT and the payoff in terms of business value. Your colleagues need to understand that reaping value from IT investments won't be instantaneous. You must communicate that and ensure everyone has realistic expectations.

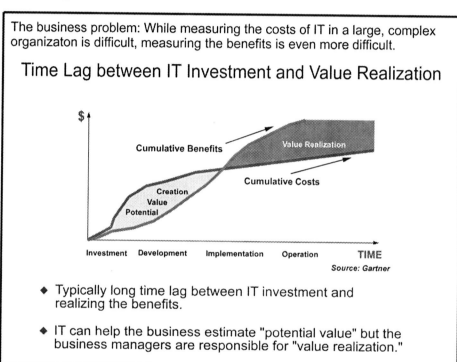

The business problem: While measuring the costs of IT in a large, complex organizaton is difficult, measuring the benefits is even more difficult.

Time Lag between IT Investment and Value Realization

- ◆ Typically long time lag between IT investment and realizing the benefits.

- ◆ IT can help the business estimate "potential value" but the business managers are responsible for "value realization."

Figure 16
Source: Gartner EXP Research – Business value, IT value: The Missing Link – November 2000 Chuck Tucker

When it comes to reaping the benefits from IT, technology managers and executives have a role to play, but ultimately it is the users of IT—people in finance, sales, manufacturing, human resources, product development, and elsewhere—who must take responsibility for realizing value. Technology alone will not boost sales, open up new markets, or create a competitive advantage. The right technology smartly applied to sound, efficient business processes and strategies will lead to success.

Now, with our road maps in hand, let's continue the journey.

Objectives, Strategies, and Metrics for Initiative 3

Mapping your IT infrastructure and applications to support your business needs.

Objectives

✥ Define an overall "Point of Arrival" for the IT architecture.

✥ Define and implement a systems-integration process.

✥ Map technology plans to support business requirements.

✥ Establish standards for each architectural component.

✥ Achieve maximum value from IT investments.

Strategies

✥ Develop and implement a technology road map to guide all IT planning and spending.

✥ Create a chart listing all business processes and supporting technology.

✥ Document redundancies and inefficiencies in your existing infrastructure.

✥ Document opportunities to support the implementation and show ROI.

Metrics

✥ Reduction in number of applications, programming needs, and servers.

✥ Reduction in time to access pertinent information.

✥ Elimination of any gaps in reliability or functionality of software.

✥ Increase in ROI through savings and cost reduction.

Initiative 4

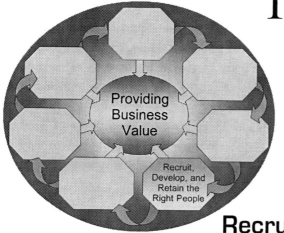

Providing
Business
Value

Recruit,
Develop, and
Retain the
Right People

Recruit, Develop, and Retain the Right Team

Building an IT Organization that Meets Your Needs

You may wonder why I've waited until Initiative 4 to talk about organization and people. The reason is simple: You won't know how you should be organized, what kind of skills are required, and how many people you will need until you've analyzed your business processes and the applications to support them, and developed the corresponding road maps to articulate your plans. Simply put, you have to know where you are going before you can assemble the team that will take you there. If you decide to construct a building in steel, you won't need many carpenters. Similarly, if you're buying and installing off-the-shelf software, you won't need a lot of developers.

Very few of us get the opportunity to build an IT organization from scratch. We usually inherit an existing staff with skills, roles, and work habits already in place. Every IT manager needs to determine if the existing organization, including its structure, skill set, and culture, are best suited to serve the company's broader goals. This Initiative will explore ways to evaluate your IT organization, define the skills and core competencies you need, and look at ways to make necessary changes to meet your goals. I'll take you through one recommended structure for organizing IT personnel (a role-based model), which clearly defines the function and responsibilities of each staff member. Then, we'll look at ways to recruit and keep top talent through such methods as a formal mentoring plan.

As IT's Role Changes, so Must Its Structure

Over the years, we've witnessed the incredible transformation of IT's role in the business world from a bit player to a chief enabler of innovation and success. That transformation has required that IT executives, managers, and staff possess a whole new range of skills outside technology; skills that include financial management, strategy development, and communications. These changes have also necessitated a reordering of the way IT is organized and managed.

Those responsible for organizing IT resources must continually assess whether their current structure best serves their company's needs. For example, some companies centralize their IT operations, coordinating all technology-related work through a single IT organization. Other companies have their IT staffs report directly to the business unit or division they support. Both approaches offer benefits and drawbacks. Your challenge, whatever organizational options you consider, is to figure out which approach best serves the needs of your business.

Business Strategy Will Dictate Organizational Structure

To determine how to best organize your IT resources, you and your IT management team should assess whether your current organization is positioned to meet your business needs—now and in the future. Noted architect Henry Louis Sullivan's observation that "form ever follows function" applies in today's business environment where strategy dictates organizational structure. Your business strategies and the requirements of your technology users should be key factors when determining the organizational structure for IT.

As you review your IT organization, there are several questions you should consider:

↳ Does your structure align with markets, customers, systems, and processes?

↳ What business issues shape your current structure?

↳ What are the core competencies of your IT organization?

↳ Who has responsibility for the strategic direction of IT?

↳ Who is responsible for best practices and costs of IT?

↳ Does your IT staff truly understand your business and the problems you are trying to solve?

↳ Do IT employees demonstrate business acumen?

↳ Do they communicate effectively with colleagues in other parts of the company and/or with customers?

Taking a Hard Look at What You've Got

The process of evaluating and organizing IT resources breaks down into several steps that all build on one another:

✥ **Evaluate the organizational structure.** How can you arrange resources, tasks, and accountabilities to improve performance? How will your organization be structured in a year? In three years?

✥ **Map the organization to the strategy.** How will your business strategy change over the next three years? What kind of IT organization will you need to successfully support these changes and put your company in the best position to achieve its stated goals, whether they are breaking into new geographical markets, developing new products, or improving productivity?

✥ **Develop the leadership you need.** What leadership qualities do you need from IT staff, now and in the future? How are you developing the necessary leadership attributes and technical competencies to meet those needs?

✥ **Create the best system for managing people.** How effectively are you acquiring, developing, managing, and rewarding members of the IT staff? What human resource systems need to be put in place or modified to meet future staffing requirements? How do you develop the necessary skills, improve responsiveness to change, and increase employee satisfaction?

Of course, accomplishing all this will take much time and effort. In fact, there may be times you feel like you have to suit up for battle when you are trying to reorganize and redirect people. But without the right staff, skills, and the appropriate organizational structure, it will be nearly impossible to achieve your goals.

Removing a Major Roadblock

One of the biggest roadblocks to any restructuring effort is usually resistance to change—whether it's changing the workplace culture or modifying long-established work routines. When change is suggested, a common response is the knee-jerk reaction of "That's not how we do things here. You just don't understand." Your challenge is to convince people to embrace change and thereby become more responsive and competitive.

So how do you bring about the necessary changes in culture, attitude, and work routines? I have found that a cross-functional, bottoms-up approach is necessary for any redesign of the IT organization, its processes, and its goals. As you undertake any reorganization efforts, I suggest organizing a task force of all potentially impacted managers working both inside and outside your existing IT organization. This way managers have a voice in the process, and soliciting their input should make it easier to win their support. In addition, if you task a single manager with accomplishing these goals, you'll likely get a modification or expansion of the current goals and organization colored by that manager's perspective. A group with broader representation ensures a wider perspective.

Before you make any major changes, your two key tasks are: educate your colleagues and earn their trust. You can't win their support unless they fully understand what you are trying to accomplish. And, likewise, you can't lead them unless they trust you and the plans you have set for them. Before you begin your reorganization, remember: communicate your plans and listen to your colleagues' concerns as you move ahead.

What Are Your Core Competencies?

Gather a group of managers together and you'll hear a lot of talk about the importance of core competencies. What does the phrase "core competencies" really mean and why is it so important? Core competencies are the fundamental disciplines that your organization must practice and master to achieve success. They are key characteristics that you decide are required at all levels of the organization. For example, in an IT organization, core competencies might be defined as application integration, business acumen, project management, communication, and leadership skills.

Defining the core competencies for your IT staff is a critical step in organizing IT resources. For instance, if you are outsourcing much of your software development work, then application development skills will no longer be a core competency for your staff. Business acumen, however, may become increasingly important as your IT staff learns the market dynamics and economic pressures shaping your overarching strategies.

Here are several examples of core competencies identified in various businesses where I have worked, along with specific and practical ideas for developing them among your IT staff. The list is intended as a starting point as you define *your* company's unique core competencies.

Business Acumen

In my talks with colleagues and other CIOs, a topic that increasingly comes up is the growing need for business acumen among IT staffers. IT organizations need people who are as well versed in business basics such as economics, finance, and business process analysis as they are in technology. Hotshot developers who don't understand the company's objectives, processes, and opportunities render themselves irrelevant by ignoring or failing to understand the company's broader business goals.

However, IT professionals who demonstrate excellent analytical skills can act as a catalyst to provoke new thinking and drive process changes. Business-savvy IT folks who understand customer needs can design solutions that map to the business problems at hand. They can become true partners with others across the company to ensure the best technology solutions are applied to the company's advantage. Technology users usually balk at accepting new systems or platforms when they don't perceive the value. IT staffers who understand users' requirements can design systems that fulfill them.

Project-Management Skills

Possessing the skills to manage projects from planning stage to completion is critical for IT staffers. As discussed in Initiative 2, skills in process and project management are vital to ensuring projects are delivered on time and on budget, and with proper documentation and metrics.

There are many ways to foster these management skills among your IT staffers. In addition to formal training programs offered by the Project Management Institute and other organizations, you can encourage your staffers to hone their skills at every opportunity. If they haven't done much project management, encourage them to take the initiative and volunteer to lead a small project to gain low-risk experience. It could be a project at work, in a professional organization, a community group, or a church. Or, they can work with a project leader as an assistant. The bottom line: IT staffers need the skills to manage a project from conception to implementation and beyond.

Technology-Integration Skills

With the variety of operating systems, platforms, development tools, and hardware systems in use at a typical company or organization, IT staffers must understand how they can all work together. A prerequisite for possessing sharp technology-integration skills is having a broad understanding of technology standards, which are evolving all the time. IT professionals can keep up with the developments through trade journals, white papers, vendor newsletters, and user conferences. There are often local or regional user groups that can be an immediate source of help, experience, and information for little or no cost. National and international user conferences provide a broader and larger pool of attendees, though they typically involve travel and registration fees. The published proceedings of the conferences can be great sources of information and are often available online.

Consulting firms like Gartner, Inc. and Forrester Research publish reports on technology integration and standards that can be particularly useful. Local colleges or universities that conduct seminars on technology integration and related topics are another good resource.

Leadership Skills

Not everyone is a natural-born leader, but fortunately, leadership skills can be learned. There are several steps you or your employees can take to build leadership qualities; some of them are very simple. Start by looking at things from different perspectives, by challenging your own assumptions. A positive attitude is an invaluable tool. Foster a culture where the attitude is "We can do this if …", not "We can't do this because …" Encourage all employees to affect change if they are unhappy with things. Encourage them to volunteer to lead efforts in your organization, such as short- or long-term projects or community-service efforts. And reward them when they do take risks and seek opportunities to learn new skills.

Both management and staff should learn more about your company's leaders and their vision for its future. Observe and learn from the leadership qualities of the company's upper management. No one can be a leader at all times. Know when to follow, and develop insights about leadership from that perspective. Seek a coach or mentor who will provide consistent feedback and advice on developing leadership skills.

Communication Skills

Communicating effectively with people across all divisions of your company as well as with customers, suppliers, and other stakeholders is critical to success. IT professionals up and down the ranks need to be able to articulate the organization's strategic direction and plans. They also must be able to listen to users' concerns, synthesize the information, then formulate solutions that meet the users' business requirements.

Many strategies exist for honing communication skills. I routinely advise IT staffers to volunteer to conduct meetings or make oral presentations, especially to "non-threatening" audiences in the community, at a professional society or organization, or for the department. I encourage them to seek opportunities to be a scribe at meetings as a way to develop listening skills and be more comfortable in front of a group. Observation is also a powerful tool, as there is much to be learned from studying the techniques of others who make presentations. Likewise, effective memos and reports can be kept to serve as models and points of reference.

As with any project or initiative, feedback is key. I suggest to IT staff members that they seek feedback from someone whose opinion they value, especially following their giving a presentation or enduring a particularly difficult situation.

A Model for the IT Organization

Once you've defined your core competencies, you'll need to consider what kind of IT organizational structure will best serve your company's needs. As you build a structure to support your company's business strategies and goals, don't put too much stock in the traditional structure of your IT organization. Instead, plan for what you want to become. Your vision and your points of arrival will determine the most logical structure and division of labor.

As part of a reorganization effort at AMD, we identified several goals that a restructured IT group needed to support, including:

↳ Improved infrastructure and support services.

↳ Increased operational effectiveness with lower costs and improved service levels.

↳ Improved quality and cycle times for product development.

↳ Better use of technology standards to minimize management complexities.

After investigating industry best practices, we decided to employ a role-based model for IT as a framework, using research conducted by Gartner, Inc. The role-based model clearly defines the roles and responsibilities for all contributors. Key components of the model included:

↳ Defining the IT services that the company required.

↳ Focusing the IT organization on delivering those services.

↳ Identifying the core competencies and leadership skills that IT needed to deliver those services.

↳ Clearly defining ownership or responsibility for each of those services.

Figure 17 is the "Role-Based Organization" model developed by Gartner. I have applied the concepts within this model at various companies, with much success. You can customize this model to fit your business requirements.

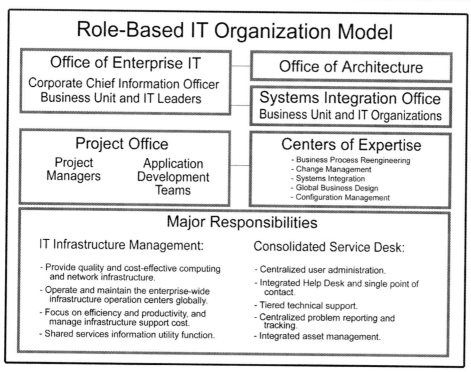

Figure 17

Source: Gartner – Using Organizational Strategy to Maximize IT Value – June 2001, Michael Gerrard

Defining Roles and Responsibilities

You may have in place some of the roles outlined in Figure 17, while others may be new to you. The key point with this model is that every person's role is made explicit, ensuring a clear understanding of who has responsibility for what. Let's look at some examples of the roles and responsibilities included in Figure 17.

Office of Enterprise Information Technology

This office is akin to a business-technology council and is comprised of the CIO, IT executives attached to the company's business units, and the executives from those business units. The CIO's role is to function as a leader, mentor, and coordinator of the interaction between the company's senior management and the IT organization. The office is responsible for developing strategic-planning guidelines; prioritizing large-scale business process, infrastructure, and enterprise-wide application projects; and reconciling conflicts over IT resources that arise between the business units.

Office of Architecture

This group has two roles. The first is to act as a repository for corporate standards, architecture, and methodology. The second is to evaluate new technologies to assess their fit within the company's broader infrastructure.

Systems Integration Office

This office acts as an advocate for the business units and their technology needs. It also has responsibility for managing relationships between IT and the business units, a subject I will discuss in the next Initiative.

Project Implementation Office

This group has a variety of responsibilities, including: establishing a standard project-implementation methodology applicable throughout the company; performing resource evaluation for new and ongoing initiatives, and completing project review and analysis to determine if goals, requirements, and budgets are being met.

Centers of Expertise

There are two main types of Centers of Expertise: Solution Delivery teams and Support teams. In general, their roles and responsibilities should include: being the single source for a particular talent or skill within the IT organization; providing skilled resources as scheduled, at competitive prices; and contributing to and complying with architectural standards.

How Does Your Organization Compare?

You can adapt the role-based model to meet your company's unique needs. That's what I have done at various companies. For example, at AMD, I introduced new management roles to augment the traditional IT organizational roles of infrastructure, application development, and applications support. These new roles included a system-architect manager, responsible for defining strategies for emerging technologies and identifying architectural limitations that might impact business directives, and a business-process management position, responsible for providing direction to management initiatives and processes. This position was also responsible for identifying best practices and cost-reduction initiatives for the IT organization that would affect the bottom line.

There are many variations on this theme and, again, the structure all depends on what business problems you are trying to solve. I've seen many innovative examples of IT executives creating new positions or even organizational structures to meet their company's needs. For instance, I recently met a CIO who added a communication specialist to his staff. The specialist's role is to promote what IT is doing throughout the company. According to the CIO, this has helped communicate the value of IT to the rest of the company.

The Next Challenge: Recruiting, Developing, and Retaining Top Talent

Once you've got the roles and responsibilities defined and an organizational structure in place, you must determine if you have a process for recruiting, developing, and retaining world-class employees. The first step is to define what characteristics you expect from employees. Are you simply looking for people with cutting-edge technical skills or do you want other qualities, too? Experience has taught me that, while technical skills are vital, other qualities such as initiative, flexibility, and commitment are just as important. Consider what qualities your employees need based on your company's business requirements.

How Deeply Skilled Is Your Bench?

It never ceases to surprise me that many companies do not have processes in place to evaluate their bench strength, the depth of skills among their existing staff. This knowledge is crucial when key personnel leave the company or are promoted to new positions. Without a succession plan, the loss of a single key staff person can wreak havoc on an organization, delaying or derailing important and costly technology projects. No company can afford that kind of risk—especially since it can be avoided with a thorough succession plan complete with recruitment strategy, a performance-review process, mentoring, and training programs.

With all the talented people out there, having a deep bench should be easy, right? Not necessarily. Many businesses do not set themselves up to succeed when it comes to recruiting and managing talent. Think about your company. Do you regularly conduct performance reviews to evaluate the quality of your employees? How soon do new managers attend management-development courses after being promoted? Do you have succession plans? If not, it's time to begin.

How Do You Assess Talent?

The chaos that can erupt with the loss of highly skilled and talented staff members can be avoided by putting in place an employee talent-review process.

Early identification and development of high-potential talent is a critical step when assembling the best possible team. A formal talent-identification process should recognize those individuals who have the greatest potential for increased responsibility. The review process should identify those high-potential individuals, describe their career paths, and provide other relevant information, such as relocation preferences and restrictions. This data will serve to identify potential candidates for open positions. The process should include a development plan that defines requirements for employees to advance, including any training needed.

Retention of top talent is an ongoing challenge. Ask any IT manager who suffered through the seemingly daily defections during the dot-com boom and they will tell you how counterproductive losing good people is. To limit such losses, you should identify employees who are at risk of leaving the company. During the review, focus on what must be done to develop the employees to their full potential and what might be done to move them through the system at an accelerated pace. That kind of planning and preparation should go a long way towards retaining desirable employees.

Recruiting the Right People

Once you have identified top talent within the company, how do you attract the best and the brightest from the outside? Any manager who has spent weeks or months trying to fill a key position knows that finding the right person for a job can be as stressful for the person doing the hiring as it is for the job candidate. You can reduce your stress by creating a well-planned recruitment and hiring process.

In my experience, several steps can streamline the recruiting process. For starters, make sure you have a clear job description to minimize the flood of unqualified applicants. Involve coworkers in the recruitment process. Make use of summer intern and co-op programs or develop such programs if they don't exist—they can be great sources of young talent. Use the company or an external recruiter, providing them with detailed information about the job requirements, such as types of degree(s), skills, and professional experience. Organize a team to review resumes collected by the recruiter. Use the Web, personal referrals, and job fairs to recruit candidates. Before you begin the interview process, develop relevant questions for the candidates. Make sure you involve human resources in the interview process.

Performance Planning

Once you assemble your team, how do you keep members motivated and satisfied? Employees who invest their time and energy in a company usually want to feel like the company is investing in them. A basic way to create this kind of work culture is through a formal performance-planning and review process. At companies large and small, I have found that the appraisal of a person's performance is fundamental to enhancing both individual and organizational productivity. Properly prepared and presented, formal performance feedback can have a positive impact on both employee commitment and performance and is an essential part of the retention process. While a formal discussion should be scheduled at least annually, encourage managers to provide feedback to employees, both formally and informally, on an ongoing basis. This continuous dialogue prevents surprises at appraisal time, something that simply should not occur in a well-managed organization.

Why Have Performance Appraisals?

Management has a responsibility to support employees by developing their capabilities, identifying their potential, and optimizing their performance. This responsibility can only be met if employees and their managers discuss the employee's job and his or her performance, wherein they can target areas for personal development or improvement that support business goals. Performance appraisals provide a regular forum for these discussions to take place.

When conducting performance reviews, the manager must sit down with each employee and review precisely what they expect from him or her. It is important that employees have input and agree with what needs to be done. This process should include metrics reviewed quarterly, which will allow you to measure the worker's effectiveness and make necessary adjustments.

Mentoring: Leadership in Action

I can honestly say that I wouldn't be where I am today without the benefit of relationships I've had with various professional mentors. For that reason, and for the life lessons, connections, and memories I have made, I've always considered mentoring a top priority. There's no better way to develop and refine your talent pool, create new leaders, and strengthen the bonds between executives and staff. A mentoring program not only promotes professional development but it also helps minimize staff turnover and boosts morale. For these reasons and many more, I strongly recommend you find a junior staff person to mentor and encourage your other executives to do the same.

How Do You Mentor?

Mentoring is a committed relationship between a seasoned professional or manager and someone less experienced in a particular profession, technology, or skill. The primary purpose is to foster professional development of the junior person through the counsel and guidance of the mentor. However, a rewarding mentoring relationship is a two-way street and should offer both parties opportunities for development and sharing of knowledge, skills, energy, and creativity.

I have done mentoring in all of the corporations where I worked and I go about the process the same way in each setting. I start by meeting as many of the most talented people in the IT organization as possible. My purpose is to select a few people I can commit to mentor. I meet with them, discuss their present job, and learn where they want to be in the next few years. I talk to them about how to work with their managers and assign projects that are of interest and challenge to them. Many people who've been part of these mentoring programs have gone on to great success, rising to key leadership positions in their respective companies.

Figure 18 illustrates the steps of a typical mentoring process:

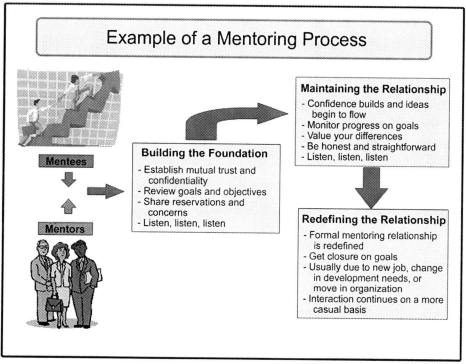

Example of a Mentoring Process

Mentees

Mentors

Building the Foundation
- Establish mutual trust and confidentiality
- Review goals and objectives
- Share reservations and concerns
- Listen, listen, listen

Maintaining the Relationship
- Confidence builds and ideas begin to flow
- Monitor progress on goals
- Value your differences
- Be honest and straightforward
- Listen, listen, listen

Redefining the Relationship
- Formal mentoring relationship is redefined
- Get closure on goals
- Usually due to new job, change in development needs, or move in organization
- Interaction continues on a more casual basis

Figure 18

In any mentoring program, whether it's a formal corporate-wide effort or an informal initiative launched individually, one must bear in mind a few basic points. Before establishing a mentoring relationship, both parties must carefully consider their responsibilities and commitments, both personal and professional. Any mentoring arrangement requires time and dedication. Developing a schedule that works for both parties will make it easier to manage the relationship. Involvement in a mentoring relationship is work, but the rewards—for both parties—can be plentiful. In addition to the professional and personal development that takes place, a mentoring program is a great retention tool, as well as a fertile proving ground for developing homegrown talent.

With the People in Place Come Relationships

Once you've assembled your team and put plans in place for leading, motivating, and mentoring the members, you'll need to think about the relationships that exist between IT and the rest of the company. The success of your IT plans and strategies may well hinge on how your IT staff relates to coworkers across the company. Next we will look at how to build the partnerships and effectively manage the relationships necessary for developing successful IT solutions within your company.

Objectives, Strategies, and Metrics for Initiative 4

Recruit, develop, and retain the right team

Objectives

- ✎ Determine optimal organization of IT resources.

- ✎ Attract, retain, and develop people to complement your existing skill set.

- ✎ Improve the professional capabilities of IT.

- ✎ Increase employee effectiveness and satisfaction.

Strategies

- ✎ Implement a process to evaluate and organize IT.

- ✎ Define and improve the recruitment process.

- ✎ Instill a business-focused, results-oriented culture.

- ✎ Establish a formal performance review process.

- ✎ Identify core competencies and map them to skill and organizational roles.

- ✎ Establish a formal mentoring program.

Metrics

- ✎ Employee satisfaction survey results.

- ✎ Percent of reductions in turnover.

- ✎ Percent of increase in promotions.

- ✎ Percent of performance reviews and appraisals implemented and completed on schedule.

- ✎ Number of staff development plans in place.

Initiative 5

Use Relationship Management to Provide Solutions through Leadership, Consulting, and Communication

Building Bridges between IT and Technology Users

While I am a firm believer in the power of positive thinking, I want to focus briefly on the subject of failure; to be specific, the failure of technology projects, whether they are storage systems, database installations, or a massive enterprise-resource-planning rollout. What IT projects can you recall that have tanked, and why did they fall so far short of the mark?

Very often, the breakdowns are not caused by technology but by human failings, such as inadequate communication or a weak partnership between the technology users and the supporting IT staff. Such failures waste time and money and usually create hard feelings and mistrust between the IT staff and technology users. These are results no business can afford.

To sharply reduce the potential risk of an IT project failing, put in place a well-defined process for managing the relationships between the IT staff and the intended users of the technology. Your objective should be to establish an open, two-way communication between the IT staff and the technology users throughout the company. This will enable IT to provide expertise and insight while they gain a firm understanding of technology users' needs. The relationship-management process will serve as the bridge between the IT organization and the business units.

Relationship management and effective communication may not sound like the typical domain of an IT organization, but they are key processes requiring skills that technology professionals must master if IT is to truly align itself with the business. You need people who can communicate the vision, the priorities, and the goals of your organization. You need people who can listen to and understand the priorities, the problems, and the needs of your technology users.

Of course, building relationships can't happen overnight. Learning about your company's technology users, understanding their needs and their goals, *and* earning their trust, takes time and much effort. Successful partnerships result from a well-coordinated process. In the following pages, I will outline a relationship-management process that will ensure that your IT organization can work in tandem with the technology users in your company and position itself to understand and serve users' needs and business goals. As with all of the Initiatives, you can adapt these suggestions to fit the needs of your organization.

Relationships Are Two-Way Streets

Building solid relationships with colleagues is a two-way street. There must be a strong commitment from everyone involved. Unfortunately, many IT organizations fail to recognize the need for well-managed relationships with technology users. That failure makes it difficult, if not impossible, to successfully execute strategies. To build real partnerships between IT and the various divisions of your company, each party must understand what the other is trying to accomplish. So, if you work in IT, you need to comprehend the goals, the problems, and the workflow of your counterparts in human resources, sales, manufacturing, marketing, and every other area of your company. If you work in one of your company's business units, you need to understand the services IT provides, as well as the skills and expertise the IT staff can offer to help you achieve your goals more quickly and efficiently.

In your experience, what kinds of relationships exist between the IT staff and the rest of your company? Do technology users fully understand how IT can support them? How often do staff from the business units meet with representatives from IT? Do discussions focus on strategic plans and the technology needed to support them? Or, instead on de-escalating tension between the business units and IT caused by a faulty application or a behind-schedule project?

Contact between IT and the business units should not happen only when problems arise. There must be an ongoing dialogue so ideas can be constantly exchanged and needs, goals, and requirements communicated. IT cannot provide support to its fullest potential without a solid partnership in place. As you move forward in building a relationship-management process, part of your challenge will be to have both the IT organization and the business units commit to developing a strong partnership. A first step in that direction is to assess your current situation.

How Does IT Relate to Technology Users?

To put in perspective what kind of relationships you currently have, start with a little introspection. If you work in IT, ask yourself how the IT organization relates to the people throughout your company who use technology to do their jobs. If you polled your company's technology users about their perception of the IT organization, would they talk about servers and applications, or would they talk about IT as a business partner and a provider of valuable consulting services?

Consider how IT interacts with other divisions of your company:

- ↳ How does IT communicate what services and expertise it can provide?

- ↳ Are there people in IT responsible for interacting with technology users, whose job it is to understand users' needs and the business problems they are trying to solve?

- ↳ When they have a technology question, problem, or idea, do people in sales, finance, manufacturing, and the other divisions of your company know who the go-to person is in IT?

- ↳ If an existing business process and its supporting applications require changes or improvements, whose job is it to communicate those changes to the IT organization and manage their implementation?

The answers to these questions and others about how IT relates to your technology users will help you build the requirements for a relationship-management process, and that process may make all the difference as to whether your company's technology investments succeed. The success or failure of your IT organization may come to be defined by how well you manage the relationships with your peers throughout your company. Without strong partnerships built on mutual respect, a deep understanding of needs and expertise, and ongoing communication, you will fail to understand what your colleagues are trying to achieve. That lack of understanding will cause your IT organization to appear hopelessly out of touch and ultimately irrelevant. You'll be like a car salesman who doesn't understand and therefore cannot communicate the features and benefits of the latest model he's trying to sell. The bottom line: lots of noise, but not much valuable information.

What Are the Benefits of Relationship Management?

Over the years, I have reaped the benefits of the relationship-management process during my tenure at various companies. In addition to streamlining interactions with colleagues, the process also helped raise awareness of the value IT provides. An effective relationship-management process can position an IT organization as a consulting practice that provides solutions to business problems, not merely as a provider of faster, bigger, better bits and bytes. I have found that users typically will go out on their own to resolve their technology problems if working with IT is too complicated and time-consuming. By carving out a consulting-practice role for your IT organization, you can help ensure that technology users turn first to IT instead of striking out on their own in search of technology products or services. This helps prevent the dreaded shadow IT projects from cropping up.

By creating a relationship-management process, which would include the appointment of account managers from IT responsible for interacting with a defined set of users, you put a *face* on the technology services your organization provides. With an account manager, someone within the IT organization *owns* the relationship with the technology users of your company and is responsible for making sure IT is accountable and responsive. By building a framework for IT to interact with technology users, you will be better able to respond to requests for new applications or other technology investments. That nimbleness can give your company a huge competitive edge in the marketplace.

In companies where I have worked which implemented a relationship-management process, I found that technology projects often rolled out more quickly because constant feedback about the initiative helped speed adoption. In addition, efforts to standardize software and hardware platforms often got a boost, since someone from IT constantly worked with the company's various business units, preaching the gospels of interoperability and standardization.

How the Process Works

The relationship-management process begins when account managers meet with coworkers from the company's business units to develop a clear understanding of the technology users' objectives and strategies. The account managers should participate in the business units' staff meetings and planning sessions. Together, the account managers and staff from the business units should translate the business requirements into technology terms to prepare for the selection of products and services.

They should clearly define the scope of all projects and determine time and financial objectives up front. Time and money should serve as regulators for technology projects to ensure articulation of clear investment objectives and identification of trade-offs.

The account manager shepherds all requests for IT investment to the IT Project Qualification Review Board, the component of the governance structure discussed in Initiative 2. This board is responsible for vetting all new project requests and plays a major role in the broader relationship-management process. The Review Board assesses the pros and cons of each request and performs cost-benefit analyses of all technology proposals. The board also prioritizes technology spending. As part of that function, the board separates "quick hitters," or high-priority projects that require relatively small investments, from more expansive requests that need more rigorous review.

Figure 19 illustrates the relationship-management process. How does it compare with what's in place at your company?

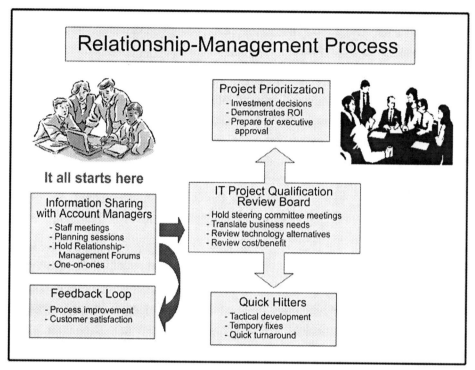

Figure 19

A Key Link: Account Managers

The account manager is the facilitator of the entire relationship-management process. This person's responsibility is to ensure technology users are satisfied with the company's IT infrastructure and the business systems and applications. Account managers must establish strong two-way communication between the IT organization and the business units. This will help foster a better understanding of technology users' business strategies and requirements, and provide insight into how technology can help solve business problems. The account manager also represents IT's interests on new projects, providing guidance on available resources, offering expertise on emerging technologies, and advocating for standardization of technology platforms. The account manager can be an executive or manager from the IT organization who has the authority to make and follow through on decisions.

The overall responsibility of an account manager is to provide IT professional consulting services to groups of technology users. The account managers are responsible for aligning technology solutions with business strategies. They contribute to the development of long-range system plans and ensure products and services are aligned with business needs. They should have the skills to conduct business-process analyses, needs assessments, develop preliminary cost-versus-benefit measurements, and communicate trends and requirements to and from customers and IT.

As you can see, the abilities and experience required of an account manager go far beyond technology skills. Business acumen is crucial, as account managers must be able to advise users on potential risks of technology investments and explain the possible impact on business processes and priorities. Communication and diplomacy skills are also vital, as the account manager must keep technology users up to date on the status of various technology projects and requests, and must keep IT executives apprised of any issues or problems that users are experiencing. This feedback can help resolve conflicts before they mushroom into large-scale problems, and help maintain a solid partnership between IT and its users.

The IT Project Qualification Review Board

Back in Initiative 2 we covered the issue of governance and the establishment of an IT Project Qualification Review Board. This board, responsible for vetting all new project requests, plays a major role in the broader relationship-management process.

Board members review new requests against work in progress and prioritize whether or not the new projects are put in the queue or need immediate action. The board also reviews "quick-hitters" or projects that can be turned around fast. The board should look for synergies across business units, uncover opportunities to share resources, and establish and review metrics on a monthly basis.

Tips from the Trenches

If your IT organization does not currently have a formal relationship-management process in place, getting one started can seem like a major challenge. It does require commitment and, in some cases, reorientation of some employees. However, the potential upside is worth the effort. Here are several tips from the trenches that may make the process easier for you.

To get the program going, start small. For example, you may want to begin by implementing an account manager program in just a few divisions of your company. This will allow you to incorporate feedback and make necessary adjustments before rolling the program out to your entire company.

In addition, consider setting modest goals at the outset. We took this tack at one company as we introduced an account manager program. From IT's perspective, the initial strategy focused on small projects that would leverage existing personnel. The plan was to complete the projects within three months, a fairly aggressive time frame, but one that helped bring quick results. Because we demonstrated the program's benefits so quickly, winning broader support of the initiative came easily.

And speaking of support, make sure you have buy-in from people at the highest levels of your company. For example, feedback about one account-manager program overwhelmingly cited support from the CIO and the CEO as a factor in the project's success. When your top executives embrace the program, it becomes easier to incorporate the entire relationship-management process into your company's DNA.

Getting the Word Out

Like any new program or initiative, you need to spread the word so your colleagues will know what you are trying to accomplish. As you prepare to launch a relationship-management process, you must consider how you will educate your coworkers both about the process itself and how it will make their lives easier. One way to do this is to distribute a company-wide announcement that outlines your plans and introduces your account managers. Letting people know is a simple but important step in building the necessary bridges between the technology organization and the rest of your company.

However, getting the word out doesn't start and stop with a company memo. It's vital to seize every possible opportunity to educate users about the relationship-management process. You can provide updates and highlight success stories about the process through company newsletters or on an internal IT web site. Planning sessions or meetings held between IT and your company's technology users also allow you to spread the word.

Change Is the Only Constant

All the initiatives described so far provide a road map for business transformation, a suggested path for changing the way your company operates to maximize performance. To transform your company and achieve optimal alignment between IT and business strategies, you must be ready and able to manage change, because change is an inevitable part of the relationship-management process.

Take a second and think about the change-management processes your company has in place. Are they formalized and well understood, or does your company deal with changes on the fly? Below is a series of sample situations that you may encounter in your own organization. As you read through them, consider what processes you have in place to handle them.

We Want More

It never fails. You just got all new systems and processes up and running and someone wants to change something.

↳ How do you handle the request?

↳ How do you make sure the request fits your goal of an optimized architecture and the "many-to-the-few" application strategy, not to mention your budget limitations and priorities?

And, if it doesn't fit,

↳ How do you convince the person or department that made the request that setting up a shadow IT project is not an option?

Growth through Acquisition

Your company has just acquired another business and now you have to assimilate all the systems: email, voice mail, finance, sales, etc.

↳ How do you handle the task of bringing completely different business processes and a new IT organization into the fold without compromising all the standards you've established?

↳ What is your strategy for getting to know the new business?

↳ How do you make sure your newest group of technology users does not become alienated in the acquisition process?

New Technology Assessment

One of your business units has outgrown its current technology and a replacement must be selected that will meet both their current and future needs.

↳ How do you go about evaluating the new technology?

↳ How do you establish appropriate criteria to review requests for new platforms or applications?

↳ What happens when you get a request for technology that doesn't fit with your overall strategy and direction?

↳ How will you evaluate new technology's impact on your overall corporate strategy?

In short, the starting point for addressing all these questions is a well-established relationship-management process based on mutual trust, respect, and strong communication. You will need to constantly review your processes and fine-tune them, and you'll have to create new ones to handle unplanned challenges and opportunities as they arise. A well-developed relationship-management process will provide your organization with the platform for two-way communication with the technology users in your company, enabling you to understand their needs and articulate all the things IT can do to help.

Communicating the Value of IT

A final key component of the relationship-management process that I've touched on briefly is communicating and marketing the value of IT. This is one of my recurring themes because it is essential for success. You must continually convey to the rest of your company the services and expertise that IT can offer, as well as the value that can be unlocked when technology investments have been optimized. For this to happen, you must keep communication open and ongoing with your community of technology users.

So how do you make this happen? Getting yourself on business executives' and managers' calendars to discuss project updates and new technology and attending their staff meetings are a just a couple of examples. I have also used an internal IT web site to draw attention to new technology products, services, and initiatives we were introducing and to highlight business-technology success stories. Other good communication vehicles are IT Project Review Sessions, where IT executives discuss the status of ongoing technology projects with the intended users, and Technology Awareness Days, where representatives from IT and key vendors set displays up in the company cafeteria to show off new products and services and discuss users' questions and ideas.

How to Convey Technical Jargon in "Big Animal Pictures"

As you communicate with the various technology users in your company, it's important to remember to speak their language. Some users may not have technology backgrounds, so you must put information in terms that are meaningful to them. You need to explain technology at a high level, in a context that users will understand to prevent their eyes from glazing over. Technical details are often boring for the average user. "Big animal pictures," or charts and graphics that reduce complex information to their simplest form, are a great way to reach people. Showing where things stand today, versus where they will be in the future, is another effective way to depict the changes that technology can effect. Figure 20 below is an example of such a slide that I have used many times.

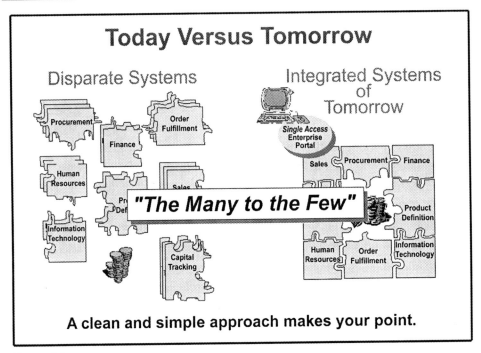

Figure 20

The possibilities for marketing IT within your company are limitless. The point is to guarantee an ongoing dialogue between IT and technology users. With such communication, you not only keep in close touch with your users, but you can also demonstrate the value of your company's IT investments. When your colleagues realize all that technology can do to optimize the business, they will better appreciate the value of IT.

Objectives, Strategies, and Metrics for Initiative 5

Use relationship management to provide solutions through leadership, consulting, and communication.

Objectives

- Provide solutions through leadership and consulting.

- Lead the way in assessing emerging technologies.

- Establish partner relationships with technology users.

- Participate in the formalization of company business strategies and solutions in support of those strategies.

- Reduce the risk in IT project implementation.

Strategies

- Implement a well-defined process for managing business relationships.

- Dedicate resources to assist business units in process definition and improvement.

- Assess emerging technologies for potential business application.

- Provide a process to train IT personnel and develop business-process expertise.

- Assign IT people as consultants to key business functions.

Metrics

↪ Number of projects with IT involvement.

↪ Projects delivered on schedule.

↪ Cycle-time reduction.

↪ Number of account managers assigned.

Initiative 6

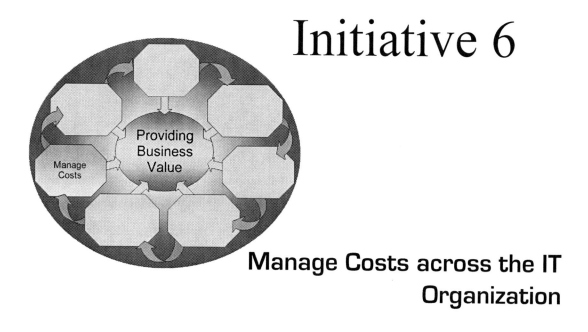

Manage Costs across the IT Organization

Justifying Every Penny Spent

In the sobering aftermath of the technology-spending slowdown, IT organizations have come under intense scrutiny. At many companies, proposed technology investments have been met with overt skepticism, if not downright hostility, from company executives who felt burned by unfulfilled technology promises—and money wasted—during the technology boom of the 1990s. In recent years CIOs have faced intense pressure to wring as much out of their budgets as possible. As a result, CIOs are increasingly expected to demonstrate the potential value of IT spending and reduce the inherent risks of technology projects.

While some indicators imply that the economy is turning around, CIOs should proceed with caution. It is doubtful that many companies will return to the free-spending ways of the late 1990s with their technology budgets. Costs must still be carefully managed, investments need to be justified, and value must be demonstrated.

As technology evolves and new business models emerge, new questions will face those in charge of IT spending:

- ✬ Are IT services a commodity or a utility?

- ✬ Should technology users be charged only for what services they use?

- ✬ What kind of competitive advantage should IT be expected to deliver?

In the following pages, I'll describe processes to build budgets that not only manage costs but also ensure that your organization can develop the necessary technology solutions and services. I'll share with you methodologies for determining the cost of services and for conducting resource planning, a critical element in building a rational and efficient IT budget. I'll also address the topic of outsourcing, specifying when it makes sense to off-load IT operations and outlining the potential benefits and disadvantages of such arrangements.

A Quick Poll

At various companies where I have worked or consulted, I usually start the budget process by posing a series of questions to the IT managers. My purpose is to obtain a basic understanding of technology users' business requirements. Here's a sample:

- ✬ Do you know and understand what technology users want and what it will cost to make them happy?

- ✬ Is your organization responding quickly enough to meet users' demands to position your company to take advantage of new market opportunities?

✎ Are your coworkers who use IT to do their jobs involved in the IT budget process?

✎ Are the costs of providing support and services rising with no identifiable increase in value or user satisfaction?

✎ Do you have processes in place to address the preceding questions?

✎ If you have processes in place, are you using them to effectively manage IT costs?

If the answer is "no" to any of these questions, then you and indeed other leaders in your company should be concerned. You'll need to determine what processes, activities, and technology you need to create a world-class organization at efficient costs.

The Challenge of Managing Costs

Many IT executives and managers agree that constant pressure to reduce IT costs can make or break the best CIOs. In recent years, that pressure has become as relentless as spam is. Support organizations like IT often face a double bind when budget season rolls around. On the one hand, they are told to cut costs; but on the other, users expect them to provide better and/or broader services.

When IT fails to provide promised service levels due to cost constraints while at the same time requesting more money to fund existing or new projects, partnerships with the business units can start to unravel. This creates frustration on all sides. A response from IT of "The money just isn't there," for an IT project is unacceptable in the eyes of many business managers. Whether it's a request for a new financial application, a manufacturing software package, or new laptops for the sales team, once employees from the business units become convinced of the need for new technology, it can become difficult—even divisive—to persuade them otherwise.

As for the frustration felt by many people in IT, as well as in many other support organizations, comedian Rodney Dangerfield sums it up with his famous quote, "I get no respect!" Sometimes, it seems that no matter what we do in IT, it is never enough to meet the demands of the technology users within our companies. I know how difficult and discouraging this situation can be; however, I believe the only way to get beyond it is for IT managers to stop the self-pity and the whining. We must instead arm ourselves with the facts and data that will help us provide quality services at the right price. That's how we will earn the respect of our peers.

A Question of Value

The level of funding that an IT organization receives often depends on the company's overall financial results. During good times, the IT organization is typically not under much pressure to demonstrate the value of technology spending. However, when budgets get tight, all eyes fall upon support organizations like IT to justify their existence. During the many times I have been through this process, I've picked up a few strategies that may also work for you.

For background, let's look at some research by Gartner. Figure 21 shows the results of a 2003 survey of IT executives covering business trends and priorities. The survey ranked the top 10 business issues facing the executives. As you can see, for three years running, the number one issue remained cost and budget pressures. According to the survey, CIOs also cited increased concerns about data security and the growing demand for faster innovation among their top challenges.

Holding down costs while investing in data security and speeding innovation (not to mention managing a wide variety of other technology priorities) can be extremely challenging even for the most talented CIOs. It's that double bind again. You're supposed to be innovative and focus on delivering services and applications that help reduce the cost of doing business and boost profits; while also being told that you need to narrow your focus and cut technology spending. It's difficult to satisfy these competing needs, but it's a challenge that ultimately can be met.

Figure 21
Source: Gartner EXP Research – Gartner's CIO's Top Ten – January 2003

Finance Wizard or Technology Expert?

All CIOs and IT managers are expected to keep pace with the rapidly changing technologies and evolving standards. On top of that, IT professionals are increasingly expected to bring financial skills and business savvy to the table. This is a trend that is not likely to go away. If you want to succeed in IT, the best strategy is to prepare yourself for the role.

All IT managers must be cost-conscious and they must work with managers in other departments in the cost-justification process. This is another instance where essential business skills can play a crucial role in demonstrating the value of IT. As covered in Initiatives 4 and 5, fundamental business acumen, along with the principles of business-process management, can help to identify and champion opportunities that reduce the costs of IT. Providing the best and most efficient technology solutions or services often doesn't depend on fancy programming skills, hyperkinetic processing power, or cutting-edge hardware. It frequently hinges on skills and expertise in accounting practices, effective communication, and sound business-management judgment; things that fall outside the traditional domain of IT. Simply put, you can't succeed in IT without these skills.

Demonstrating Value

Across all industries, in companies both large and small, many IT organizations struggle to demonstrate their value and market themselves as enablers of business success. Many CIOs fall short when it comes to providing quantifiable data that shows the impact of technology investments.

There are traditional metrics that technology executives use, such as measuring IT costs as a percentage of total sales revenue, which can run counter to the precept of investing in IT for the future. As an example, tying IT funding to a business's overall sales revenue can become an inhibitor during economic downturns just when it is typically easier to cut better deals with hardware and software suppliers.

IT is not alone in this dilemma. Talk with corporate executives in other support organizations like human resources and finance and you will hear a common theme: when it comes to corporate-wide cost reduction, such departments are usually among the first to be scrutinized. Any division or department that does not produce revenue or which doesn't have data to demonstrate a positive ROI will likely feel the pressure.

So what approach should you take when the budget crunchers set their sights on your organization? The foremost thing to remember is that you must focus on creating and demonstrating value, not simply on cutting costs. Demonstrating value, putting the costs and benefits of IT spending into context for your business, is a much greater challenge than simply slashing accounts. When it comes to IT, your company expects robust, reliable applications such as email and Internet access, but how do you determine the value or ROI of such things? How can IT provide metrics to show the advantage of the email system? Does the system improve productivity for the business and/or reduce the cost of paper? Who is responsible for tracking this data and determining ROI? When you develop strategies for measuring the costs and benefits of IT investments in partnership with your colleagues who use those investments to do their jobs, you are taking a major step forward in demonstrating the value that those investments add to your company.

What's Your Cost-Reduction Strategy?

Given the economic conditions that have shaped the business environment in recent years, most IT managers are familiar with the question: What's your strategy to reduce costs?

A first step is to determine your core competencies. As an example, what technology services do you keep in-house and which do you outsource? Is your IT organization best at providing business solutions or coding? Do you plan to implement out-of-the-box technology? If so, should you consider shedding those legacy services to focus instead on supporting your company's key objectives? What can you do to shift fixed costs to variable costs?

New approaches to drawing up your budget may shed light on the impact of potential budget cuts. One tactic is to develop a series of budgets that clearly demonstrate the effects of different funding levels. For example, a Level One budget might reflect the amount of money needed to maintain the services you currently have running; a Level Two budget would show what's needed to provide operational upgrades planned as part of lifecycle replacement or are included in your technology road map; and a Level Three budget would include projects that span the enterprise and will require capital expenditures and participation from the company's various business units. This type of budgeting clearly shows the CFO or other senior management how funds will be used and what will be achieved.

As you try to wring excess costs from your budget, you must examine all available tools, such as systems-management software and remote-applications support, that you can be use to drive operational efficiencies. You should consider initiatives such as server consolidation to reduce the total cost of ownership for your infrastructure. You should evaluate repetitive or non-strategic functions such as help desk and application support as candidates for outsourcing. What about shadow IT? Centralizing any IT-related activities being run outside of IT's purview may bring efficiencies as well. Another key step is to identify and manage IT costs by their rate and volume components, such as cost-per-user or cost-per-mailbox. This will help immensely when evaluating services.

What Do You Know about Your Costs?

In an ideal world, CIOs would obtain the funding they request because of the central role IT plays in enabling the company to achieve its goals. Unfortunately, that's not reality. In the real world, IT organizations often struggle to defend their spending requests each time the budget cycle comes around. For any IT manager, a key part of preparing for the budget process is determining, down to the penny, what it costs to run IT. You must be able to slice and dice expenditures far beyond the traditional *labor* and *non-labor* categories. You must have processes in place to quickly determine the cost of services like email and the help desk so you can compare them to what outside service providers charge.

Over the years I developed a model to review costs. It's a simple approach, but it has proven effective in budget discussions with executives at various companies. It includes examining three components: cost drivers, levers, and initiatives. Drivers are those factors that cause you to spend money on technology, such as: the number of technology users you support, the amount of data and network traffic you handle, the number of customized applications, the speed of data access required, and the number of servers deployed. Levers are inexpensive, relatively simple steps you take to contain costs. They might include server consolidation, renegotiating contracts with suppliers to get more favorable terms, or leasing hardware instead of buying it. Finally, cost-management initiatives are broader, more expansive measures that typically require capital outlay. Such initiatives include introducing compression technology to reduce network traffic, instituting voice-over IP to lower phone bills, or re-engineering business processes to use off-the-shelf software instead of requiring custom applications that match your processes.

Here's an example of how I typically use this approach: For starters, I talk to the company executives about what drives IT costs—and this discussion is usually an eye-opener. Many people who work outside IT have no idea what it costs to provide the technology services they need to do their jobs. If, for instance, the company was trying to rein in email costs, we might look at such cost-drivers as the extra storage array purchased to hold all the outdated email that users hoard. Next, I would discuss a corresponding lever, such as limiting the size of users' mailboxes to help control costs. And finally, we would explore related initiatives, such as the implementation of the latest email technology, equipped with filtering, calendaring, and collaboration features, which would introduce efficiencies and, thereby, bring down costs.

By examining every aspect of IT in this way, you can provide a detailed list of all your costs and have at hand a full understanding of the options you have to control them.

How Do You Look at Costs?

I belong to several CIO roundtables and they each meet a couple of times a year so members can discuss common issues and challenges. These meetings provide excellent opportunities to look behind the curtains at other companies and see how they are applying IT to improve their businesses. In our discussions, we usually compare budgets, sharing our strategies for planning and spending.

At these gatherings, I am always curious as to how other CIOs approach managing the costs of IT. To satisfy my curiosity, I've done some informal polling to better understand what services these IT executives provide, how much their services cost, and what metrics they use to measure their value. What I typically find is that IT budgets are broken out into the following categories: labor, telecommunications, maintenance and repair, depreciation and amortization, travel, building allocation, and miscellaneous. In my experience, however, such traditional IT accounting falls short in many ways. For example, what if you need to know the total cost of providing email? How about the cost-per-mailbox or cost-per-email sent? What is the cost to operate the help desk? What is the cost-per-response from the help desk? Without ways to break out these costs, you can't really determine which services you're providing efficiently and which ones you need to reassess. My approach is to break out my budget by type of service. In this way I can pin down the cost of these services accurately and quickly, and provide precise answers to tough questions about costs and efficiency.

Figure 22 is an example of how I break out and review the cost of services that IT provides. For instance, I have identified at least 11 services in the area of infrastructure alone. The first column shows the service provided. The following columns show the description of the service and components, such as labor and non-labor, which includes the cost of hardware, software, depreciation, etc. Once you know your costs, you can compare them to what service providers charge and benchmark yourself against what your peers at other companies are spending. This will give you the quantitative information you need of the strengths and weaknesses of your IT organization and thereby provide hard data as you sit down with your colleagues in finance to discuss the budget.

Example of Menu of Services for Infrastructure

Type of Service	Description	HC	Labor	Non Labor	Total
Corp IT Operations Support	24x7 operations support for business applications computing environments				
Electronic Information Security	Intrusion detection, anti-virus, email and Internet filtering, modem management				
LAN Connectivity	LAN, WLAN - Data/Voice/Video				
WAN Connectivity	WAN - Data/Voice/Video				
Server and Storage Administration	Hardware management, event monitoring, capacity and performance management				
Help Desk	24x7 Help desk operations				
Business Continuity Planning, Disaster Recovery	Manage the business continuity planning process				
Email and Calendaring	Administration of corporate electronic mail systems				
Client Productivity Tools	Develop desktop and laptop images, administer Microsoft back-office applications (SMS, IIS, ISA Terminal Server)				
Desktop/Laptop Break Fix	Install new client systems and resolve client trouble tickets and work requests				
Management and Administration	Staff Managers, administrative assistants, office space				

Figure 22

What Happens when You Reduce Service Levels?

When there is no alternative but to cut costs, what processes do you have in place to determine where you should direct your reduced IT investments? Do you have a plan for assessing the net result of reduced service levels or the impact of completely eliminating the service? To address these issues, I developed a prioritization process that includes my colleagues from other parts of the company. Using the list displayed in Figure 22, we rank the services that IT provides in terms of what are most important to the users. I then use those rankings to discuss with my colleagues how budget cuts will impact the services. By depicting the priorities of the services in a top-to-bottom listing, I can show what services would be lost or reduced as a result of the cutbacks.

At one company where I worked, it quickly became apparent that in today's world of hackers, worms, and viruses, security needed to be the company's No. 1 technology priority. To support this conclusion, we also used research from Gartner, displayed in Figure 23. Such outside research can be a useful guide when setting budget priorities, and in your discussions with executives outside of IT.

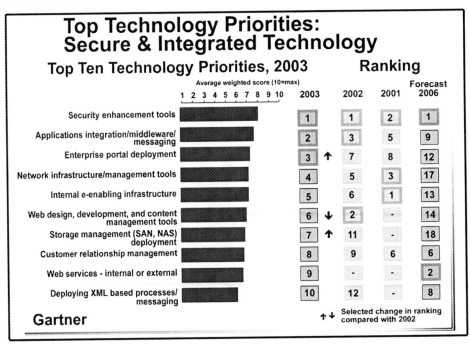

Figure 23
Source: Gartner EXP Research – Gartner's CIO's Top Ten – January 2003

When I sit down with my colleagues in finance and other areas of the company, I always address the possibility of reduced service levels, describing the potential impact so they fully understand how reductions will affect their business processes. For instance, questions I typically explore with them include: "What if we reduce the level of phone service, which results in a dial tone every other time you pick up the receiver? What if it takes five hours to get an email, or what if we limit the size of email messages you can receive or send to a line or two?" Describing the potential impact in such terms gets the message across.

How Do Your Services Compare?

Looking at costs by type of service is a useful tool for assessing where your company stands in terms of how much it spends on IT services. To gauge how my company stacks up, I break out the costs by type of service and compare the numbers with costs of similar services provided by other businesses and by IT service providers. It's useful to know how you benchmark against other IT organizations, as well as what's considered best of breed by research firms.

Figure 24 shows how I draw the comparison. Best-of-breed companies or businesses are those that have proven to be the most efficient in delivering the particular service you are evaluating. Gathering this data will probably require some research on the Internet or making some phone calls. Best-of-breed data should be available from outside research firms or through trade magazines.

Examples of Service Level and Cost Comparisons

Type of Service	My Company IT	Other Providers Benchmarks	Best of Breed
Email Service Level Cost/mailbox	99.99% $3.50	99.0% $5 - $25	99.0% $5.00
NT Servers Service Level Cost/user	99.98% $10.12/mo	99.0% $14.88/mo	99.0% N/A
PC Cost/user	$49	$62 - $94	$71

Figure 24

99.9% versus 95%

It may sound counterintuitive, but when assessing IT priorities in the context of your budget limitations, you should ask yourself if a service level of 99.9% is too high. It just may be. Let's say you have traditionally strived to provide 99.9% network uptime. What would happen if you reduced your goal to 95% uptime? How much money could you save? How would the costs of the added downtime compare to the cost of achieving "Six-Sigma" perfection? Would it be worthwhile in the long run, especially considering your business needs and strategies? It may sound strange, considering the trend in business management circles to strive for perfection, but you'll never know unless you review the numbers.

Consider this example: The network components responsible for shipping products may need 99.9% uptime. Payroll, on the other hand, probably just runs every two weeks, so it may work just fine with 95% uptime. Remember that you don't know what you don't know, so it can't hurt to take a look.

Dismantle the Shadow IT Projects

Technology projects and staff outside the company's centralized IT organization can be a major cost driver. As covered in the previous initiatives, these shadow IT projects evolve for various reasons, but the challenge for IT is the same: to secure ownership and accountability of all hardware and software applications within the company. The bottom line is that there is a cost benefit to the consolidation of both hardware and software. When shadow IT projects exist, duplication in headcount, servers, maintenance, and licenses usually exists, too. Streamlining these operations can result in significant savings.

To accomplish the elimination of shadow IT you may have to challenge and dismantle the various independent IT fiefdoms that have developed. You'll never have complete control of IT if you don't bring these renegade projects and services into the fold. Any consolidation efforts can get tricky if people feel like they are giving up control, so a first step is to meet with managers whose divisions run those projects to gain their trust and, ultimately, their support.

Throughout the course of my career, I have heard strong arguments on both sides of the shadow IT debate. For instance, several CIOs I know report that people in their companies have set up their own Intranet sites outside the IT department. These Intranet sites usually needed minimal up-front investment and were rapidly deployed by non-IT staff. The groups that set up these Intranets were generally of the opinion that the sites should be maintained and supported outside of IT because of the need for constant changes and updates.

To convince your colleagues that this kind of arrangement is untenable, you must be able to show the cost and impact of each additional server plugged into the network without your knowledge. How should the help desk react when it receives a call about problems with hardware and software that no one in IT knew existed? You need to make available the facts and figures that show the additional support costs incurred when rogue software persists in your standardized environment.

How Many DBAs are Needed to Change a Line of Code?

One of the best ways to prepare for the budget cycle is through a thorough resource-planning process to determine the facts and data that will justify the staffing and funding levels necessary to accomplish your goals. Without an effective process for projecting what you need, it will be difficult to make your case for the money and staff you require. For example, do you know how many database administrators (DBAs) you need to support your database systems? Do you know how many calls your help desk fields per day and the average time it takes to resolve each call? If you don't know or can't articulate this information, it will be difficult to convince your corporate finance managers to approve the funding you need. And remember, very few CIOs get blank checks these days. Every penny spent must be justified.

Here's an approach I use in the resource-planning process: I start with a basic model of 21 work days per month, with 8 work hours per day, for a total of 168 work hours per employee month, for each employee. From that number, I deduct hours for vacation and holidays to get a base of approximately 132 work hours per employee per month. (This number, of course, may vary from business to business, depending on: length of workday at the company, vacation benefits, etc.). With that monthly base, you can establish a formula to project workload hours. For example, if you expect an IT project to take 280 hours to complete, then it would take one person working full-time two months, or two people working full-time one month. This might sound like straightforward math, but the key is that both CIOs and managers from the business units must agree on the length of the project, as well as the amount of resources required to complete the work.

Another important area where resource planning comes into play is unplanned developments like the acquisition of a new company or the launch of a new business. IT must be fully engaged in these events, or the risk of failure increases dramatically. If IT is not involved in resource planning early, when these situations arise, costs often get overlooked. The expense of integrating business systems like finance and human resources as well as integrating email, phone systems, and other connectivity costs, are frequently not accounted for. These and other hidden costs can hinder or derail the whole endeavor.

The best way to represent IT is with knowledge of your resources and your operations. You should know how to estimate how many hours it takes to complete a project or how much it costs to deliver various services. Knowing this information and being able to communicate it to your colleagues will keep you on track to achieve results on time and within budget.

We Can Save You Millions!

"We can help you cut costs!" or "We'll save you millions!" How many times have you heard such offers, whether in cold calls or unsolicited email? Ironically, one of these offers may be valid. The last thing you want to do is to miss an opportunity that might save you a significant amount of money. These pitches contain a lot of information and, to be sure, a degree of hype. I could spend a good chunk of my day trying to make sense of what the vendors are trying to sell. So, how do you separate good products and services from timewasters? Every IT organization needs a formal process for vetting these offers without dragging down productivity.

Below is a process to sort through product pitches and offers. I call it the Methodology for New Opportunities. It states the business problem, objective, and strategy for sizing up the pitches.

Methodology for New Opportunities

The Business Problem:

- ↳ There is a constant stream of proposals/products claiming to save us millions.

- ↳ Most do not pan out.

- ↳ Each proposal/product needs resources to review and validate claims.

- ↳ Looking at each one as they come in would stop all productive work.

Objective:

- ↳ Identify and select those that may apply to our business.

- ↳ Keep running at maximum productivity.

- ↳ Get the maximum benefit from the offers that make sense.

Strategy:

- ↳ Cycle through each proposal when the existing contracts come up for review.

- ↳ Put proposals into a process that ensures a full review.

- ↳ Have knowledgeable staff review selected opportunities and proposals.

What about Outsourcing?

Outsourcing is a hot-button issue in today's environment for a variety of reasons, generating passionate responses from people on both sides of the issue. Controversy aside, outsourcing has become one of the most popular ways to cuts costs. Although outsourcing has gained much attention recently, the practice has been around for years and comes in a variety of shapes and sizes. It may mean expanding a relationship with a business partner or supplier by paying that partner to come on-site and run particular operations for your company, or it may mean contracting with a company to run your IT operations off-site, sometimes overseas where labor is cheaper.

Regardless of the special arrangement, a lot of preparation must go into a decision to outsource. Implementing an outsourcing strategy can be extremely complex as it touches on such sensitive issues as labor, security, and privacy. It requires well-documented business processes, established relationship-management practices, and a thorough knowledge of your costs.

Before entering into any outsourcing relationship, you must clearly define the reasons for doing so. For example, are you outsourcing to enhance the quality of service? To lower costs? To address staffing issues? Or are you trying to focus entirely on your core competencies?

An important first step is to define a very explicit set of goals. These will help identify the advantages and disadvantages of outsourcing.

Reducing Expenses

At one company where I worked, the initial conclusion was that an outsourcing move would reduce expenses because the vendor had less expensive labor and processes that were highly effective. We began looking at outsourcing only portions of IT, like application support and help-desk support. We concluded that outsourcing only parts of the IT organization would be more expensive than outsourcing all our IT operations because the vendor wouldn't be able to achieve economies of scale and other efficiencies with a piecemeal approach.

Outsourcing should take into account *all* costs of the IT functions—both corporate IT and the hidden cost of supporting shadow technology projects. When evaluating an outsourcing deal, you must also consider start-up costs, transition costs, and the ongoing expenses of the contract. Start-up costs (Your finance organization will categorize these as transition costs.) can make the first years of an outsourcing agreement more expensive than retaining the work in-house.

Focus on Core Competencies

As I previously stated, a question you must repeatedly ask yourself is "What are our core competencies?" Do they include designing state-of-the-art integrated applications? Or are they providing an infrastructure based on leading-edge technology and processes to achieve low cost?

If support for some services, such as help desk or application support, is available through outsourcing at an affordable price, there is no reason to keep them in-house. Why not move the support functions to companies with best practices and processes? By shedding these services, IT management can focus resources in areas that add value to your company's core competencies. Spending time maintaining infrastructure can also distract the IT organization from developing capabilities to communicate and to help them work more effectively. Both can have significant impact on the company's bottom line.

Staffing Issues

We can all agree that the IT employment market today generally favors employers. But not long ago, the tables were turned. During the Internet boom, most businesses had trouble recruiting and retaining technology professionals. The recruitment and hiring process took up a huge amount of time and energy for many IT executives and managers. A question to consider is: Do you want to manage people and be responsible for staffing?

A quality outsourcing vendor can offer strong advantages in staffing. I have found that outsourcing vendors usually have been able to support their claims of low employee turnover, even in the toughest labor markets, and they always seem to have sufficient depth to cover any spot losses. Further, an IT professional working for an outsourcing vendor has a career in a company that depends on that individual for its profits. The employee is not in a support organization but is part of the company's core competency. Not having to recruit, interview, and hire staff can have a huge impact on an IT manager's job by freeing time for activities that have much more potential benefit.

Outsourcing Should Not Be Taken Lightly

Over the years, I have seen companies make both smooth and difficult transitions when they began outsourcing contracts. Outsourcing should not be taken lightly and the more effort you put into it early in the process, the greater the potential for success. At the outset, you need a deep understanding of the business problem you are trying to solve. For instance, is your goal to reduce costs, improve effectiveness, or both? You need to know how effective your current processes and support are, and understand the potential for improving them through outsourcing.

A superficial analysis of potential outsourcing deals will not suffice. You must look behind the numbers to fully understand how outsourcing will impact your bottom line. For example, outsourcing costs may often be higher in the short term because transition costs can be steep, depending on how long it takes to transfer support to the vendor and eliminate staff positions. These costs can be managed down in the long term, once you reduce head count and the outsourcing vendor introduces efficiencies.

If you decide to outsource some or all of your IT operations, take great care in developing the Request for Proposal (RFP) for the vendors. Your company should benefit from long-term cost reductions, so if your vendor realizes savings, your company should share in those savings. Such stipulations should be included in the RFP.

To help analyze the pros and cons of outsourcing, I have found it wise to hire a consultant with expertise in planning and evaluating outsourcing proposals, as well as choosing a vendor. At one company, we attempted an outsourcing project on our own and quickly discovered how complicated the task could be. We ultimately realized we did not know what we did not know and hired a consultant to help. The consultant evaluated our project plan, our existing processes, and their effectiveness. He concluded that our schedule was too aggressive and that our staffing plan for the project was light. He made a valuable recommendation to draft a baseline assessment of our existing services to compare with the outsourcing vendor's service levels.

See for Yourself

In addition to the routine checking of reference accounts, I suggest visiting the outsourcing vendor's support locations as part of the due-diligence process. It's important to see the operations for yourself. These visits fundamentally changed *my* views on outsourcing because, in many cases, the vendors' capabilities exceeded my expectations. On several occasions, I came away from the site visits convinced that the vendors could provide IT infrastructure services of a much higher quality than my company's IT organization. The vendors' entry-level skill requirements were higher, their staff's collective expertise was deeper, and their work was process-driven and thorough.

Managing the Relationship

If you outsource any or all of your operations, your role will change from managing technology to also managing the relationship with the outsourcing vendor. This is a big shift, one that will test the effectiveness of your relationship-management skills and processes.

As you move forward, it is important that both your staff and your vendor know who the relationship managers are—if your staff has a complaint or suggestion about the services being provided, they must know whom to contact. Similarly, the vendor must know who to contact on your side to ensure communication in the other direction. Managing the outsourcing relationship can make or break a company's objective to reduce costs, and a successful relationship manager for an outsourcing initiative must possess both technical savvy and business expertise to ensure objectives are met.

What's the Bottom Line?

Entire books could be written on the subjects of managing costs and the pros and cons of outsourcing; both topics are so multifaceted and complex. Hopefully, the information I condensed in this Initiative will serve as a starting point as you look at managing costs in your own company.

Of course, no one-size-fits-all plan exists for cost management in business. I would suggest that you carefully examine the solutions I have listed, then take these ideas and shape them into your own.

For many CIOs, successfully meeting the challenge of managing costs will define whether they succeed or fail at their jobs. Looking ahead, it's impossible to know how economic conditions will evolve. However, you can be certain that even as corporate IT investment rises, the demand for demonstrable ROI will not abate. CIOs will continue to feel the pressure to justify their costs down to the penny.

Managing costs does not necessarily mean reducing spending. It means making sure all IT investments are made wisely and that they deliver maximum value to your company. With sound processes in place for evaluating costs and assessing the many tools available to manage them, you will be able to optimize the investments your company makes in IT.

Objectives, Strategies, and Metrics for Initiative 6

Manage costs across IT.

Objectives

↳ Identify and champion opportunities to reduce IT costs company-wide.

↳ Ensure a best-value IT cost structure.

↳ Manage costs to stay within the budget.

Strategies

↳ Implement tools to drive operational effectiveness.

↳ Model approaches to reduce the total cost of ownership for IT assets.

↳ Evaluate non-core competencies for potential outsourcing.

↳ Evaluate all functions for cost effectiveness.

↳ Identify and evaluate IT-related activities performed outside of the IT organization (shadow IT).

↳ Identify repetitive, inefficient, or non-strategic functions for potential outsourcing.

↳ Identify and manage IT costs into services components.

Metrics

↳ Staying within budget.

↳ Per-user cost reductions.

↳ Operational cost savings.

Initiative 7

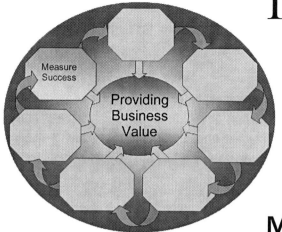

Measure Success

Providing
Business
Value

Measure the Success of Your IT Strategies

Are Your IT Investments Paying Off?

The previous six Initiatives of this book covered a lot of ground, including understanding the business requirements of technology users, developing and implementing sound business processes, devising a governance structure for managing IT strategies, building sound relationship-management practices, assembling the best team, and managing costs. Now, we've come to the capstone of all that work—measuring the success of your IT strategies.

When I think about this topic, the first thing that comes to mind is my favorite quote: "You don't know what you don't know." In other words, it's impossible to gauge whether all the money your company spends on IT is paying off until you actually measure the results. Just as relevant to this initiative is its corollary: "You may not know what you think you know." The point is, you can't assume anything, especially when it comes to technology users and their level of satisfaction with the tools the IT organization provides them. Too often, those of us in IT assume technology users are happy with the software, hardware, and support we deliver. Unfortunately, this is often not the case.

When it comes to satisfying your users, take nothing for granted. You can't base any of your work on assumptions or you will increase the risk of your IT investments failing. Your objective must be to keep users happy by meeting or exceeding their expectations. To accomplish that, you have to take the pulse of your users on an ongoing basis, and have processes in place ready to react.

The process of measuring the success of your IT investments must be based on a true partnership between IT and the technology users in your company. What you decide to measure must be defined in terms of what is relevant to users. As with IT work, technology users and their needs must be your focus.

Establishing Satisfaction Metrics

The first step in measuring the success of your technology investments is to define what will be measured. As you do this, bear in mind that the metrics must be meaningful to your users, not only to those in IT. You may have spent millions of dollars upgrading servers to ensure 100% uptime of your systems, but unless there are quantifiable benefits for your users, the investment will prove irrelevant. Reducing production costs, shortening the length of the sales cycle, or speeding up product delivery are the kinds of things far more meaningful to your users than the features of upgraded applications or servers. Robust applications or cutting-edge hardware will mean nothing to technology users unless they perceive a tangible benefit

As you define what you will measure, the relationship-management process again plays a key role. IT account managers, or whoever is responsible for IT's relationship with that particular division or department of the company, must work with users to devise a set of metrics relevant to both the business units and to IT.

An increasingly common example that results from this process is the Service Level Agreement (SLA), a pact between the IT organization and a division or group of users that outlines the scope of the work to be provided and defines expectations for service and support. These documents also spell out management and communication plans as well as performance measurements. An IT organization may have SLAs with each business unit or division within their company.

I have found that SLAs are great tools for managing and measuring IT value. The agreements articulate the users' needs and expectations and define what IT will do to meet them. A nice benefit from the SLA process is that a closer relationship between IT and technology users usually develops. When technology users see how IT is helping them to accomplish their goals and objectives, they will better understand the business value of the company's technology investments.

Figure 25 from Gartner shows how a measurement system can clearly link business value with IT investment. For instance, if a company is trying to speed up product development to become more competitive, it should measure the time it takes to move the product from concept to commercial availability. IT comes into play by enabling all involved parties—from the people inside the company to external partners and suppliers—to work collaboratively. IT's role in this process can be judged by the reach of its infrastructure and the services it provides to support the necessary collaboration. As you can see, these metrics are driven by business needs, not technology.

Some Examples of Evidence Trails from Business Values to IT Value Indicators

Linkages

Business Value	Business Measure	IT Value-Add	IT Value Indicators
Faster to Market	Elapsed time from concept to availablity	Support for collaborative design both internally and externally	◆ Reach of infrastructure internally and externally ◆ Range of collaborative services supported
Higher Reliability	Defect rates for new products	In-service monitoring for early warning; ability to correlate multiple data points, batch/lot tracking	◆ % of products covered by in-service monitoring system ◆ % of products covered by batchtracking sys.
Better Cross-Selling	Cross-selling ratio	Easy access to integrated product and customer information	◆ Quality and use of product and customer data supplied to salespeople
Reduced Customer Wait Time	Product/service delivery time	Dynamic scheduling of resources	◆ Reduction in product/ service delivery time
Reduced Cycle Time	Elapsed time for common activities	Automation of repetitive business processes; creation/ redesign of business processes	◆ % reduction of cycle time for IT-dependent processes ◆ Expand to processes that are IT-dependent

Figure 25
Source: Gartner EXP Research – Business Value, IT Value: The Missing Link – November 2000 Chuck Tucker

A Program for Action

The process of measuring IT investments doesn't end with a list of metrics. An action plan for making improvements is also necessary. To accomplish this, many businesses use the Balanced Scorecard approach. Developed in the early 1990s, the Balanced Scorecard is a management system that examines a variety of value-drivers within an organization and provides feedback on both related processes and outcomes. This allows an organization to make continuous improvements. A plethora of consulting practices, books, conferences, and software tools are available to help develop Balanced Scorecard systems. I have found this approach to be an extremely useful tool.

If your company is not engaged in a Balanced Scorecard effort or other management system that provides a vehicle for measuring success and making improvements, I suggest you advocate for one. Whether you work in IT or elsewhere in your company, you can provide leadership by pressing for such a program. The important point is that every company or organization needs a program for action—one that allows it not only to measure its strategies and processes, but also puts it into position to make continuous improvements.

Consider Your Technology Users as Customers

As you begin the process of measuring your IT strategies, you must consider a few questions: Do you really know how happy technology users in your company are with the services that IT provides? Is your IT organization prepared to do whatever is necessary to keep your users satisfied? Do you think of your users as *customers* and treat them as such?

Treating your company's technology users as customers—not just as coworkers that make demands on your time for service and support—is an important step to providing high-value IT services. Terms like being "customer-centric" and having "customer focus" are common themes in today's business environment because of the rich upside of having a close alignment with the parties with which you do business. In all the companies where I have worked, focusing on customer satisfaction has always been included in the overall corporate objectives, strategic plans, and bonus schedules. If you think of your users as customers, it's more likely you will be highly attuned to their needs and more committed to fulfilling them.

To satisfy technology users, the IT organization must keep in close touch with their needs, goals, and habits. To accomplish this, I recommend development of a survey process that allows IT to gather ongoing feedback, whether it's about a new ERP application, upgraded laptops for the sales team, or the responsiveness of the help desk. Those in IT must be aware of what users think.

The survey process will allow you to methodically gather data, analyze it, and then take actions to make necessary improvements. Surveys can provide snapshots of where the IT organization stands and help identify organizational weaknesses.

As this process unfolds, consider whether you have identified metrics that will address areas such as:

↳ **Quality** – How good are the services that IT provides?

↳ **Quantity** – Is IT offering all the services users expect and need?

↳ **Responsiveness** – How responsive is the IT organization to users' requests, problems, and concerns?

↳ **Timeliness** – Do users get support from IT when they need it?

↳ **Flexibility** – Is the IT organization sufficiently flexible so it can adapt to unforeseen conditions?

↳ **Adding Value** – Is technology improving the ability of users to do their jobs?

↳ **Cost of Service** – Are the costs of IT services reasonable?

How Long since Your Last Checkup?

When was the last time you surveyed your technology users to get their views on your company's IT organization? If it has been more than a year, I would highly recommend that it's time to check again. The old saying "out of sight, out of mind" applies here: if your users don't hear from you, they'll never fully understand or appreciate all you do for them. No one in IT can afford to lose touch with the technology users they serve.

User surveys often point out disconnects between the way users view IT and the way the IT organization views itself. I have witnessed many instances where IT personnel were surprised to find out that users did not understand all that their IT organization was doing to support them and did not appreciate the value that IT added to their business. In many user surveys, feedback indicated that users felt IT focused too much on operations, rather than on helping with the strategic direction of the company. Of course, we in IT don't particularly like to hear this, but we must face the facts.

A Wake-up Call

At one general meeting of my IT organization, I asked the staff to estimate the satisfaction level of our company's technology users. Without hesitation, they overwhelmingly expected that 85% to 100% of the users would express a high-level of satisfaction with IT. A few months later, we conducted a survey of technology users and to our surprise, only 40% of the respondents were completely satisfied with IT, while another 45% didn't have an opinion one way or the other. The remaining 15% of the survey respondents were not at all happy with IT's services. After all the hours spent rolling out new applications, providing 24/7 support, troubleshooting hundreds of problems, and making what we considered significant progress toward achieving our goals, who in the IT organization would have guessed that our users would rate us so much lower than our own expectations?

I must say that these particular survey results caused more than a little consternation. What were we doing wrong? After reviewing the survey data and write-in comments, the short answer was that we hadn't fully educated our users on our business value and the breadth of services we offered. Users knew that we existed and spent a lot of money, but they wanted IT to better understand and support their business needs and to communicate better with them. Users also expressed a desire for better responsiveness and timeliness.

As a direct result of the feedback, we decided to implement an improvement plan that would first focus on the 45% of users who had not yet formed an opinion and convert them to satisfied customers. We also put in place a plan to keep the existing 40% of satisfied customers happy. As for the 15% who had a negative view of IT, that took many one-on-one meetings to determine the source of their displeasure. When we took the survey again six months later, I was delighted to discover that 75% of the respondents were satisfied with the level of service they were receiving from IT and only 5% were still not happy. We were making progress.

Planning the Survey Process

So where do you start when you want to roll out a user survey? Research houses like Gartner and Forrester have done a good deal of work on user satisfaction surveys and have excellent information that can get you started. Much information is also available on the Web. You have available a variety of methods such as email, the Internet, or telephone surveys; you will have to pick the one that best fits your budget and your needs. There are short, specific queries that can yield useful results. At some companies the help desk includes an online questionnaire at the end of their trouble tickets to assess how well problems were handled. Of course, participation was strictly voluntary so as not to extend the time users were involved in the problem-resolution process. The questionnaire was brief, but it provided valuable information about the users experiences with one of IT's most important services.

The most formal survey is the professionally prepared online or paper questionnaire. Questions are specific and asked a few times in different ways to ensure accuracy of the data. If your budget allows, I would recommend this method.

You will also need to decide the timing, frequency, and sample of the survey. Some may be conducted annually and company-wide, while others may be fielded at the end of a project and directed at a specific user base involved with the project. Experts in survey research suggest your questionnaire be user-friendly and easy to return to create the best odds for a high rate of participation.

Surveys can be staged in phases. For instance, a first pass might be a broad satisfaction survey to determine the overall perception and understanding of IT's operations and services; the second phase, developed after the initial round of data has been analyzed, could focus on specific services and issues.

I recommend that surveys be done regularly, regardless of the medium or method. Figure 26 displays an example of an overall process flow, beginning with the development and administration of the survey. The key to this process is that it is "closed-loop," where strategic and operational planning feedback is incorporated to ensure continuous improvement.

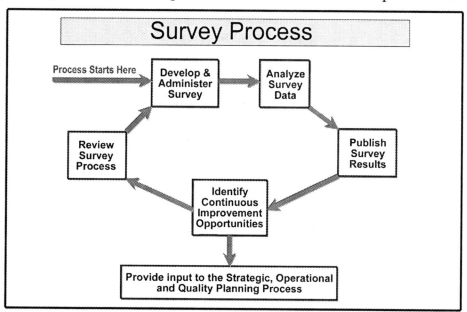

Figure 26

Introducing Your Survey

How you introduce a survey can generate interest and encourage participation. The old saying that you only get one chance to make a first impression applies here. Remember, you are asking people to take time to participate. I have found that users will be more likely to step up to the plate if they understand from the outset what business problems you are trying to identify and solve with the questionnaire.

The following is an example of a letter I have used to introduce a web-based survey to users:

> Dear Technology User,
>
> As a service organization, the IT group is always in continuous improvement mode. To help achieve our goals and to better support you, we are soliciting your feedback which will help us plan significant improvements over the next two years. Within the next month, you will have an opportunity to evaluate IT as a whole, including the services and products offered, through a web-based survey. This survey will help us better understand what aspects of the IT group are helpful, along with those you feel need improvement.
>
> The survey will run from April 15 through May 15. We will send you an email with the survey URL embedded in it. You just have to click on the link to access the survey.
>
> You will have the option to provide feedback on IT as an organization, as well as the various departments and services within IT that you regularly contact or use.
>
> Your responses will be kept completely confidential. As an IT organization, we must stay competitive and with your help, we hope to provide the best possible technology and services to you.

Once the data has been collected, we will evaluate the findings and develop steps for future action. All survey results will be published directly to you and on the IT web page. We anticipate making the survey process a key component in our planning cycle.

Please let us know if you have any questions. Thanks in advance for your participation and for your comments and suggestions.

Sincerely,

IT Management

Provide Prompt Feedback

Once you get people to answer your questionnaire, your work is just beginning. A crucial part of the survey process is to ensure the results don't end up in a black hole. Think about it: What better way to alienate respondents who have taken time to provide thoughtful answers to your questions than to ignore their remarks and suggestions? The survey sets a level of expectation that you must meet or exceed. You must get results back to the participants as quickly as possible and describe what actions will be taken to address their concerns. A lack of timely response can do more damage to your relationship with technology users than not conducting the survey in the first place.

Don't wait for someone to ask for results. One vehicle for delivering quick feedback is via email. I suggest releasing survey data in stages. For example, in the first wave, you can thank the participants and release the high-level results. In the next communication, you can give them drill-down data complete with action plans and specific steps you'll take to address their concerns. Be as candid as possible and let participants know what you can and cannot do. You need to set realistic expectations for what changes and improvements will be coming. If some things cannot be acted on in the near term, like ripping out and replacing the corporate email system, you need to explain why.

Analyzing the Feedback

As you analyze the survey results, you will have to prioritize users' concerns. The survey should include a list of items participants can rate in terms of the importance to them versus their level of satisfaction. It makes sense to first take action on what the user feels is most important, especially if there are many concerns and areas of dissatisfaction.

The following is an example of such a list from a survey I conducted early on at AMD. The IT staff developed the categories in collaboration with users.

The categories, which described the IT staff and which users had to rate, were:

- Effective communications
- Flexibility
- Overall technical support
- Reliability
- Responsiveness
- Supports business needs
- Timeliness
- Understands business needs
- Provides added value

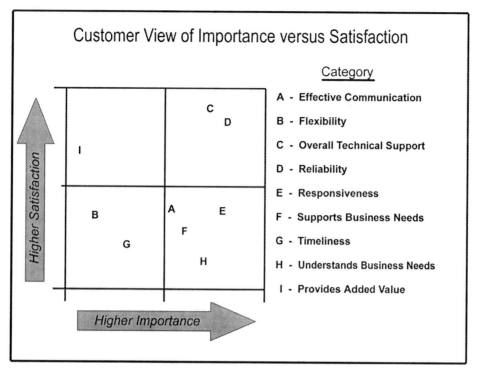

Figure 27

Figure 27 displays how we used the survey results to prioritize users' responses. Axis X depicts the level of importance the user placed on each item while the users' collective satisfaction level is displayed on axis Y. As you can see, the categories of the highest importance to users and that were the most satisfactory to them were overall technical support and reliability. Meanwhile, the categories that registered low satisfaction but high importance to users were those shown in the lower right quadrant: effective communication, responsiveness, supports business needs, and understands business needs. This gave us a clear picture of how to establish our priorities and set the stage for developing improvement plans.

Plans for Improvement

Once you've analyzed the survey results and identified the areas on which to focus, you need to develop improvement plans that address users' concerns. In all my years of participating in and conducting user surveys at different companies, some common concerns usually emerge: a lack of responsiveness, poor communication, and questionable reliability. It is imperative that you address these issues and that you communicate your action plans.

Getting the IT staff together and breaking down this information so that everyone accepts the results is the first step to putting together an action plan. You may need to invite some of the survey respondents to meet with the IT staff to help clarify their comments and to assist with the improvement plan development. This should only be done if the respondent has identified themselves and stated a willingness to discuss these issues.

One time, during a customer satisfaction feedback and improvement planning session, it came to light that some IT employees did not know what services our organization offered. How could we market our services and communicate effectively across the company if the people working in IT didn't understand the scope and breadth of their responsibilities, skills, and initiatives? We decided then that our first step would be to clean our own house and educate the IT organization on all of our ongoing support and projects. To accomplish this, we implemented project-review sessions open to all IT staffers so they could get up to speed on all the initiatives underway within IT.

Taking Action

Your improvement plans should clearly and concisely spell out the steps you will take to address concerns identified in the survey. The following items come from an action plan I developed and put into place based on survey feedback.

To address the need for better communication between IT and the business units, IT will:

✎ Implement an IT Quality Feedback Hotline and web page for users to offer comments, suggestions, and concerns.

✎ Implement a process to ensure guaranteed follow-up to users on any complaints or feedback.

✎ Conduct quarterly communication meetings to give users the opportunity to ask questions and receive updates on IT programs and initiatives.

✎ Distribute a monthly newsletter throughout the company with information about IT plans and accomplishments.

To provide better service and support we will:

✎ Improve the trouble-ticket and hotline follow-up process.

✎ Implement a single point of contact for all IT issues.

✎ Improve responsiveness to users' requests through reduced turn-around time and increased sensitivity to business needs.

✎ Meet or exceed Service Level Agreements.

To improve support for users' business needs, IT is implementing improved project-management practices including:

✎ Creating a formal project-review process so IT can communicate project status to users.

 ✍ Publishing all project road maps and plans on the internal IT web site, which is available to all users.

 ✍ Building consensus between users and the IT organization through better project prioritization and justification methodology.

 ✍ Communicating regularly to users about project deliverables, schedules, changes, and the impact of changes.

Each of these examples had detailed plans on how they would be executed, managed, and measured, and I assigned IT leaders to carry them out.

Surveys Only Show Part of the Picture

Awareness of users' needs and perceptions doesn't end with the survey process. There are many ways to gather feedback. All of them can provide invaluable information about how users are faring with the tools that IT provides. You should always have your feelers out. For example, occupying a seat at the company tables of power to provide input to strategic plans, set expectations, and receive feedback is one way to influence user satisfaction. Having account managers conduct informal interviews with users about what they expect from IT, as well as holding quarterly feedback sessions, can both be useful vehicles for gathering information. Simply walking around your company and having conversations with people at all levels of the organization can provide key insight into the business problems that users are facing and how technology is helping or hindering them. Inviting users, including key managers from your company, to have breakfast or pizza with the CIO is a great way to share information and take stock of users' concerns.

Keeping IT Users Happy

So how does an IT organization consistently keep technology users satisfied? One recurring message I have heard over the years is that users want a better relationship with IT. That begs the question: How do you build and sustain a strong working relationship between the IT organization and technology users? The answer isn't solely in the quality of technology services provided but in the basic character of the relationship and in both parties' willingness and ability to be flexible, innovative, and committed to fulfilling expectations. That requires a common language and common yardsticks for understanding, measuring, and communicating business needs and value.

Another message I have heard throughout the years is that users want doing business with IT to be easier. While they may enjoy and respect the functionality of the hardware and software that IT provides, they often struggle with the processes—or lack of processes—in place for working with IT. While these challenges may be steep, they are certainly not insurmountable.

Let's face it. Sometimes it's easy to keep our heads in the sand and believe everything is rosy with technology users. The truth is, taking action to improve user satisfaction can lead to greater accountability, shouldering of additional responsibility, and having more work to do. However, in all my years in IT management, I have found that keeping technology users happy is one of the most critical elements in establishing IT as an enabler of business success. After all, what better measure of success is there for an IT organization than satisfied technology users?

Objectives, Strategies, and Metrics for Initiative 7

Measure the success of your IT strategies.

Objectives

- ⌘ Enhance the value of IT by establishing a measurement process.

- ⌘ Establish metrics that are relevant to users.

- ⌘ Improve satisfaction of technology users.

Strategies

- ⌘ Create feedback channels such as regular surveys and user satisfaction forms.

- ⌘ Implement a process to clearly define service-level agreements and metrics.

- ⌘ Provide prompt feedback to technology users.

Metrics

- ⌘ Increased user satisfaction.

- ⌘ Service-level reports.

- ⌘ Increased participation among users in surveys and other feedback opportunities.

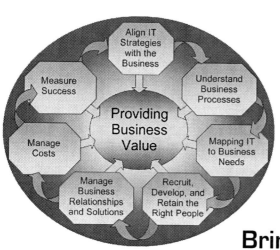

Summary

Bring the Initiatives to Life

Words into Action

We have now come full circle. Taken together, the Seven Initiatives for Creating and Understanding a Professional IT Organization should provide a framework for mapping IT investments to business strategies. Bringing the initiatives to life is a matter of taking action, creating or modifying business processes to support overarching organizational strategies and goals, and executing the plans you have crafted.

As we all know, there is often a great chasm between concept and execution. A lack of efficient processes, a shortage of resources, and poor communication can easily derail the best plans. Experience is a great teacher, and my 35 years in the IT profession taught me many lessons at companies both large and small. While each company or organization is unique with its own culture, goals, strategies, and human dynamics, many universal characteristics are shared by all businesses, government agencies, and nonprofit organizations. Here's some advice about putting the initiatives into practice.

Start at the Beginning

By now you must know that a guiding principle of mine is: you need to understand the business problem you are trying to solve before you throw technology at it. Whether the underlying challenge is to boost customer retention, increase sales revenue, or streamline manufacturing, you can't begin to plan improvements until you fully understand the problem. One of my biggest nightmares as a CIO is being called into a meeting to address such issues before objectives are clearly defined and articulated. In such situations, the upshot is that people usually voice a lot of opinions, many of them not related to the problem at hand. As a result, people walk away without any idea of what needs to be done to move forward. This breeds frustration, fosters a sense of futility, and ultimately leads to failure.

Without exception, the starting point for all my work is sitting down with colleagues from the various business units or divisions of my company to discuss what their priorities are and what obstacles are impeding their success. All the work that IT needs to do will flow from there.

It is important to understand that the Seven Initiatives are all interconnected. While they provide value collectively as well as individually, they are meant to be taken as a whole. I would strongly suggest that you not stray too far from the process sequence I have laid out. For example, I would not recommend undertaking Initiative Four, recruiting and retaining staff, until you have developed an understanding of your company's business processes and devised a supporting technology road map.

A Review

Before outlining some tips for success, let's review the Seven Initiatives:

Initiative 1: Align IT strategies with your organization's vision, objectives, and business strategies

Remember, technology investments will be futile if they do not serve your organization's overarching goals and visions.

Initiative 2: Understand your company's business processes so you can optimize IT's role

Before you can plan business improvements through technology, you must analyze and understand how your organization operates and what processes it employs to accomplish its goals.

Initiative 3: Mapping your IT infrastructure and applications to support your business needs

To get maximum value from IT investments, a company's technology infrastructure must support current and future business needs. A well-developed road map for an integrated and open IT architecture can guide all technology spending and deployment.

Initiative 4: Recruit, develop, and retain the right team

Assembling a committed, highly skilled group of technology professionals encompasses a great deal more than simply placing employment ads. Developing effective leadership skills, fostering business acumen, and establishing a mentoring program are just some of the steps required to build a successful team.

Initiative 5: Use relationship management to provide solutions through leadership, consulting, and communication

You can reduce the inherent risks of an IT project's failing by putting in place a well-defined process for managing the relationships between the IT staff and the intended users of the technology.

Initiative 6: Manage costs across IT

IT managers are facing increased pressure to justify every cent they spend on technology. Thorough resource planning and cost management are some of the tools available to ensure you deliver the necessary technology solutions and services.

Initiative 7: Measure the success of your IT strategies

It's impossible to know whether all the money your company spends on IT is paying off until you actually measure the results. Every IT organization must work with technology users to develop relevant metrics to gauge the value of their IT investments.

Tips for Success

In the introduction of this book I covered a few ground rules. Here I reiterate some of them.

Responsibility

Each initiative must have an owner, someone who assumes responsibility for bringing it to fruition. With responsibility comes accountability, and that helps assure the initiative will not fall through the cracks. Ultimately, the initiatives should become part of the culture of your IT organization.

Involvement

Involve users in the development of all technology projects. As you plan and build new applications or platforms, you should involve the people who will use them every step of the way so the features and functionality meet their needs.

Support

Get backing from your company's senior management team for all Seven Initiatives. Top executives can help build broad support for the Initiatives and provide insight about the overall direction of your company.

Flexibility

Remain flexible. Business conditions constantly change, executives leave, mergers and acquisitions occur, new technologies emerge, and market opportunities develop. IT strategies and the professionals who manage them must be ready to adapt.

Execution

Execute on all the Initiatives. The best-crafted plans in the world are rendered meaningless by lack of execution. Instead of being a vehicle for success, plans and initiatives that never get off the ground become useless shelfware that only serve as a reminder of unrealized potential.

So What's the Problem?

Over the years, I have found a few basic formulas lead to success. One primary example is:

Good people + a good plan + support from the business = success.

If the path to success is so clear-cut, then why do so many companies lose their way? I have witnessed many companies failing to achieve their goals not for lack of vision or strategies but simply because they failed to execute. In their book, *Execution: The Discipline of Getting Things Done*, Larry Bossidy, the former chairman of Honeywell International, and Ram Charan, business consultant and an advisor to CEOs, describe execution as not merely tactics but a system of getting things done through questions, analysis, and follow-through. Execution, the authors maintain, is the bridge between strategy and results.

What separates organizations that execute successfully from those that don't? Some colleagues and I developed a list of attributes and conditions that differentiate an action-oriented organization from one that fails to execute its plans and strategies. Figure 28 displays some of the items on that list. In which column does your company belong?

Action-Oriented = Execution

Action-Oriented

- Quick and decisive decision-making. Understanding it is better to move forward than to wait for all the answers.

- The ability to leverage existing investments whenever possible to develop cost-effective, flexible, efficient solutions.

- Decisions based on quantifiable customer data whenever possible.

- All interactions are conducted in the spirit of cooperation, not driven by internal competition.

- Respect for and adherence to established business processes.

- Communication is truthful, candid, and frequent, and is directed at people in all levels and business units within the organization.

Lack of Execution

- Business opportunities are squandered because of indecision or inability to commit to solutions or projects.

- Excessive costs incurred because existing investments are not fully leveraged.

- Solutions do not support business needs.

- Lack of teamwork creates poor morale and ineffective use of resources.

- Processes fall short of meeting goals and objectives.

- Poor or infrequent communication leads to redundant efforts, divisiveness between business units or divisions, and weakened partnership between colleagues.

Figure 28

Change and Flexibility

As technology continues to evolve and new business models emerge for the delivery of IT products and services, many companies are at a crossroads with respect to their IT strategies. The great debates rage on about the value of IT and whether IT services should be considered a core competency or if they should be outsourced. Still more questions fuel the fire: Is IT a commodity? Should technology services be considered a utility with a pay-as-you-go pricing structure?

As these issues play out, perhaps the most pressing question for IT organizations remains: How do businesses maintain long-term IT investments as they struggle to meet short-term financial commitments? I firmly believe companies will be successful only when they begin to use IT as a strategic weapon throughout their businesses and not simply view IT's role as supporting email and servers. While IT can offer powerful tools to help advance business goals, the ability to use those tools effectively will depend on the strength and flexibility of the relationship between the IT organization and those who use technology to do their work.

To meet all these challenges head-on, IT organizations must be ready to adapt to the changing demands of the technology users they serve. In business, as in life, we all face uncertainties. A single market disruption can throw even well-prepared organizations into chaos. Over the years, I have learned that the Seven Initiatives, really a system of interconnected business processes, can help steer a company through such uncertainty. By incorporating these Initiatives into an organization's DNA, a company can position itself to deal with the unexpected. Whether it's the entry into a new market, the acquisition of another business, or a change in company leadership, having well-defined processes in place will help any company continue executing on goals and strategies. Far from being a rigid formula to be followed, the Initiatives are a framework that you can adapt to fit the changing needs of *your* organization.

About the Author

Fred Mapp has more than 35 years of experience in the information technology (IT) profession, having held key executive positions at IBM, InfoSpan Corporation, American Express, Honeywell, and AMD. He was instrumental in the development and implementation of new technology applications and services and in the re-engineering of the IT organizations in all these companies. He has extensive experience in cost reduction and outsourcing in the IT organizations he has led.

In May 2004 he was named CEO/President of the World Congress on Information Technology 2006, an organization that brings together global leaders of business, government, and education to direct the future of technology and drive social and economic development.

Mapp also launched his own consulting business, Quality Service Solutions, to help companies identify their business requirements and develop processes for key technology products and services, such as sales force automation, customer resource management, enterprise resource planning, and e-business applications. He specializes in the areas of process management, RFP generation, and vendor selection and implementation. He has provided consulting services to a variety of Fortune 1000 and software companies.

Over the years, he has been involved with several process-improvement initiatives, including ISO9000 and Six Sigma programs. In 1990 while at IBM, he successfully implemented quality-improvement systems and process-change management disciplines, leading one of the support organizations recognized with the coveted Malcolm Baldrige Quality Award.

Mapp is a motivational speaker and frequently presents to companies how they can improve business processes and implement technology to achieve a sustained competitive edge. He has been a guest speaker at CIO conferences and numerous industry seminars. He has also been featured in articles in *CIO, Fortune, Black EOE Journal, Diversity Careers, InformationWeek, Optimize* and other publications. He established the web site www.mapping-it.com, a source of information for those involved in the development and execution of business and technology strategies.

9 780974 562445